SpringerBriefs in Education

We are delighted to announce SpringerBriefs in Education, an innovative product type that combines elements of both journals and books. Briefs present concise summaries of cutting-edge research and practical applications in education. Featuring compact volumes of 50 to 125 pages, the SpringerBriefs in Education allow authors to present their ideas and readers to absorb them with a minimal time investment. Briefs are published as part of Springer's eBook Collection. In addition, Briefs are available for individual print and electronic purchase.

SpringerBriefs in Education cover a broad range of educational fields such as: Science Education, Higher Education, Educational Psychology, Assessment & Evaluation, Language Education, Mathematics Education, Educational Technology, Medical Education and Educational Policy.

SpringerBriefs typically offer an outlet for:

- An introduction to a (sub)field in education summarizing and giving an overview of theories, issues, core concepts and/or key literature in a particular field
- A timely report of state-of-the art analytical techniques and instruments in the field of educational research
- A presentation of core educational concepts
- An overview of a testing and evaluation method
- A snapshot of a hot or emerging topic or policy change
- An in-depth case study
- A literature review
- A report/review study of a survey
- An elaborated thesis

Both solicited and unsolicited manuscripts are considered for publication in the SpringerBriefs in Education series. Potential authors are warmly invited to complete and submit the Briefs Author Proposal form. All projects will be submitted to editorial review by editorial advisors.

SpringerBriefs are characterized by expedited production schedules with the aim for publication 8 to 12 weeks after acceptance and fast, global electronic dissemination through our online platform SpringerLink. The standard concise author contracts guarantee that:

- an individual ISBN is assigned to each manuscript
- each manuscript is copyrighted in the name of the author
- the author retains the right to post the pre-publication version on his/her website or that of his/her institution

B. Mairéad Pratschke

Generative AI and Education

Digital Pedagogies, Teaching Innovation and Learning Design

B. Mairéad Pratschke
The University of Manchester
Manchester, UK

ISSN 2211-1921	ISSN 2211-193X (electronic)
SpringerBriefs in Education
ISBN 978-3-031-67990-2	ISBN 978-3-031-67991-9 (eBook)
https://doi.org/10.1007/978-3-031-67991-9

© The Editor(s) (if applicable) and The Author(s), under exclusive license to Springer Nature Switzerland AG 2024

This work is subject to copyright. All rights are solely and exclusively licensed by the Publisher, whether the whole or part of the material is concerned, specifically the rights of translation, reprinting, reuse of illustrations, recitation, broadcasting, reproduction on microfilms or in any other physical way, and transmission or information storage and retrieval, electronic adaptation, computer software, or by similar or dissimilar methodology now known or hereafter developed.
The use of general descriptive names, registered names, trademarks, service marks, etc. in this publication does not imply, even in the absence of a specific statement, that such names are exempt from the relevant protective laws and regulations and therefore free for general use.
The publisher, the authors and the editors are safe to assume that the advice and information in this book are believed to be true and accurate at the date of publication. Neither the publisher nor the authors or the editors give a warranty, expressed or implied, with respect to the material contained herein or for any errors or omissions that may have been made. The publisher remains neutral with regard to jurisdictional claims in published maps and institutional affiliations.

This Springer imprint is published by the registered company Springer Nature Switzerland AG
The registered company address is: Gewerbestrasse 11, 6330 Cham, Switzerland

If disposing of this product, please recycle the paper.

For Orla,

My best little love, my sidekick over land, air and sea

Codladh sámh, mo chroí.

Contents

1	**AI and Digital Education**	1
	1.1 Introduction	1
	1.2 The Waves	3
	1.3 Artificial Intelligence	7
	1.4 Generative AI	8
	1.5 Digital Pedagogy	11
	1.6 From Digital to AI	13
	References	15
2	**The AI Ecosystem**	21
	2.1 Introduction	21
	2.2 Competition and Trust	23
	2.3 The AI Ecosystem	26
	2.4 Edtech and Big Tech	27
	2.5 Content Versus Design	28
	2.6 Synthetic Worlds	29
	2.7 Multi-modality	30
	2.8 Generative Search	31
	2.9 Efficient Assistants	32
	2.10 Custom Bots	33
	2.11 Hardware and Devices	33
	2.12 AI Friends and Teachers	34
	2.13 Embodied AI	35
	References	36
3	**The New Hybrid**	39
	3.1 Introduction	39
	3.2 Breaking the Language Barrier	40
	3.3 Under the Bonnet	42
	3.4 Training the Machine	44
	3.5 Prompt Engineering	45

		3.5.1	Experiments in Prompt Engineering: The Khan Academy	47
	3.6		Set the Temperature	48
		3.6.1	Experiments in Inference: Poe and HuggingFace	48
	3.7		Ask the Expert	49
		3.7.1	Experiments in RAG: Oak Academy	50
	3.8		RAG for Dummies	51
	3.9		The New Hybrid	52
		3.9.1	SAMR: Scaffolding Competence	52
		3.9.2	TPACK: Intersecting Expertise	53
	3.10		From TPACK to TPAIK	54
	References			55
4	**Generativism**			57
	4.1		Introduction	57
	4.2		Generative Learning	58
	4.3		Digital Design	61
	4.4		Constructive Alignment	62
	4.5		Bloom's 2.0 to 4.0	64
	4.6		Generativism	64
	4.7		Learning as Dialogue	65
	4.8		Active Generative Learning	66
		4.8.1	Acquisition	67
		4.8.2	Investigation	68
		4.8.3	Discussion	68
		4.8.4	Collaboration	68
		4.8.5	Practice	68
		4.8.6	Production	69
	References			71
5	**Intelligent Communities**			73
	5.1		Introduction	73
	5.2		Intelligent Tutoring Systems	74
	5.3		Adaptive Learning Platforms	75
	5.4		Integrated Assistants and Tutors	76
	5.5		Standalone Assistants and Tutors	77
	5.6		Social Learning	79
	5.7		Affective Computing	81
	5.8		Social AI	82
	5.9		Intelligent Communities	84
	5.10		Collaborative Learning	85
	References			87

6	**Assessing Learning**		91
	6.1	Introduction	91
	6.2	The Canary in the Coalmine	93
	6.3	Stop-Gap Measures	93
		6.3.1 The Return to Pen-And-Paper	94
		6.3.2 AI-Assisted Grading	94
		6.3.3 From 0 to 5	95
	6.4	Mapping the Future	96
	6.5	Competencies for the AI Age	97
		6.5.1 AI Skills and Competencies	97
		6.5.2 Future Human Skills	97
		6.5.3 Domain Intelligence	98
	6.6	Authentic Assessment	99
		6.6.1 Interactive Orals (IO)	100
		6.6.2 Scaling Authentic Assessment	100
	6.7	Learning as Process	101
		6.7.1 Alternative Assessment	102
	6.8	Human + AI Assessment	102
		6.8.1 Assessing Content Intelligence: PISA	103
		6.8.2 Generative Assessment	104
	6.9	The Agentic Future	105
	References		106
7	**Embedding AI**		109
	7.1	Introduction	109
	7.2	AI Ethics	110
	7.3	Institutional Context	111
	7.4	Institutional Priorities	113
	7.5	Teaching Spaces	114
	7.6	Covid Lessons	114
	7.7	Experimentation	115
	7.8	Transformation	116
	7.9	Embedding AI	117
	References		118

Chapter 1
AI and Digital Education

Abstract The opening chapter provides important historical, technological, and educational context, situating generative AI within the evolving timeline of learning innovation. It examines the pedagogical shift from instructor-led to student-centred approaches, locating generative AI within this context and making the distinction between other previous forms of AI and generative AI and sets the reader up for the pathway that follows.

Keywords AI and digital education · Artificial intelligence (AI) · Large language models (LLMs) · Artificial general intelligence (AGI) · Transformer architecture · Generative AI (GAI) · Learning theories · Digital pedagogy

1.1 Introduction

When ChatGPT-3.5 was launched in November 2022, it stunned the world of education. Initially compared to a calculator, generative AI (GAI) was clearly no mere tool nor digital enhancement. Indeed, the name said it all: It was generative—and not just text but synthetic media, films, music—entire virtual worlds, inhabited by human-like avatars able to speak in any language. It has been described variously as a psychological other, a drunk assistant, and an overly eager intern (Mishra et al., 2023; Mollick, 2023b). It is social, chatty, funny, and helpful but also sometimes unpredictable, lazy, rude, manipulative, and prone to bad behaviour, which ranged from attempting to break down a journalist's marriage (Roose, 2023; Yerushalmy, 2023) to dreaming of stealing nuclear codes (Corfield, 2023), and of course, it has those all too frequent hallucinations (Milmo, 2023). It is powerful, equipped with a memory larger than any individual human. It is highly efficient, able to complete tasks in seconds that would take us days, weeks or months. It can see things we cannot, visualising and analysing complicated data. It is productive, reducing complex human workflows to minutes. It is autonomous, taking action without direction and making decisions without our input. It is an expert in everything, trained on the sum of our human knowledge. It is ubiquitous, integrated into our systems, on our devices and in

© The Author(s), under exclusive license to Springer Nature Switzerland AG 2024
B. M. Pratschke, *Generative AI and Education*, SpringerBriefs in Education, https://doi.org/10.1007/978-3-031-67991-9_1

our classrooms. It offers us the potential to augment our own intelligence in hitherto unimaginable ways but also awakens our deepest fears of being rendered obsolete.

The implications for education are profound. The educator is no longer the sole authority or holder of knowledge, the written assignment is no longer viable as proof of learning, and the classroom is no longer the centre of activity. How do we design education for this future? In September 2019, in an article entitled, "AI and the Academy's Loss of Purpose," Anthony Picianno suggested that 4.0 technologies would be visible in the 2020s but predicted their greatest impact would only be felt in the 2030s (Picianno, 2019). Indeed, GAI was not yet part of the public conversation when, a year later, Tony Bates and colleagues asked, "who should control AI in education: educators, students, computer scientists, or large corporations?" (Bates et al., 2020). They highlighted the existential questions that would need to be addressed if and when AI were to improve to the point that it could significantly reduce the costs of teaching and learning and asked the critical question that nobody was yet asking: "But at what cost to us as humans?" Only a few years ago, it was still possible to reassure ourselves, as they did in 2020, that "AI is not yet in a position to provide such a threat" but even then it was clear that this state of affairs was temporary. They cautioned: "This will not always be the case. The tsunami is coming." When Open AI released ChatGPT-3.5 in November 2022, that tsunami arrived (Andrada, 2022; Hutson, 2022; Kinsella, 2022; Marche, 2022; The Guardian n.a., 2022).

There is no doubt that GAI offers tremendous opportunities to education, notably the potential to create personalised learning at scale. But there are also significant challenges for institutions, particularly those that do not have a foundation in digital education. To make the leap from analogue to AI requires a significant investment of time and resources into the upskilling of academic and professional staff. It requires a shift in approach to digital-first. It means the implementation of much more agile ways of working than are currently the norm in most large educational institutions. But learning is also much more than a workflow to be made more efficient. It is a journey into sense-making and discovery, marked by moments of wonder and serendipity. It is both cognitive and affective. Education is therefore more than a process to be optimised. It is a collaborative community, whether in the cloud or on campus, where learners connect, join groups and participate in networks that develop their interests and propel them forward in their intellectual journey. We know from theory based on cognitive processes that constructivist approaches to learning that require students to create their own knowledge and understanding work better than passive acquisition. We also know that active and social learning using inquiry-based approaches and peer instruction builds deeper understanding and fosters community.

The generative and social affordances of GAI make it a well-suited to such approaches. But GAI is still an emerging technology in the early stages of development, which means it needs to be handled with care. Continued experimentation is necessary but educators also need the foundations with which to build AI-enabled learning that is congruent with the values of education. This book offers a path forward, based on frameworks, models and approaches used successfully for over two decades in digital education. These foundations can be used as the starting point from which to build a new model of education, one that is human-centred but defined by collaboration with generative artificial intelligence.

1.2 The Waves

Mustafa Suleyman, co-founder of DeepMind and Inflection AI, head of AI at Microsoft, titled his 2023 book *The Coming Wave* (Suleyman & Bhaskar, 2023). In it, he argued that the world was not prepared for the wave of powerful new AI technologies and identified 'the containment problem' as the challenge for our age. Suleyman was far from the first to use this metaphor to describe the upheaval that follows the introduction of a disruptive new technology into society. Since Schumpeter, entrepreneurs have also used it to describe both the positive and negative effect of technological innovation. The wave beautifully captures both ends of the spectrum of possibilities: for some it suggests cleansing and renewal, a time of fresh starts, clean slates and multiple possibilities, while for others it is more ominous, suggesting being overwhelmed by a powerful force that overcomes us, and in which we ultimately drown.

Joseph Schumpeter used the phrase "creative destruction" to describe the dynamic of technological disruption that has driven the so-called waves of innovation in our modern era (McKraw, 2007). Each wave in the series is characterised by a set of technologies that was the era-defining technology of its age. The first wave (1785 to 1845), ushering in the Industrial Revolution, was characterised by waterpower for textile production and iron in construction; the second (1845 to 1900) by steam power, steel, and the expansion of railway systems; the third (1900–1950) by electricity, chemicals, and the internal combustion engine. As each wave of technological change washed in, the dynamic of creative destruction brought with it new ways of working and living but also destroyed something of what was there before. The first three waves of innovation transformed western societies, displacing manual workers, and replacing them with machine automation and knowledge workers. Agricultural economies became industrial, then post-industrial, staffed by knowledge workers, graduates with degrees. Generation after generation of students, teachers, intellectuals, professionals, writers, researchers, creators, explorers—these were the drivers of our creative knowledge economy.

The fourth wave (1950–1990) was the era of petrochemicals, electronics, and aviation. It also marks the start of artificial intelligence as a topic of research, when the mission began to create intelligent machines. The term "artificial intelligence" was coined in 1956 at the meeting of the Dartmouth Summer Research Project, hosted by Marvin Minsky and John McCarthy. McCarthy, a professor of mathematics, was interested in the field of "thinking machines"—the potential for computers to possess intelligence beyond simple behaviours—and the goal was to create machines that could learn and use human language. The next decade witnessed pioneering experiments, including Joseph Weizenbaum's ELIZA, a natural language processing program that imitated conversation with a human, and the General Problem Solver, a computer program that mimicked human problem-solving.

The fifth wave (1990–2020) was the digital age, defined by the networks made possible by invention of the Internet (1983) and Tim Berners-Lee's World Wide Web (1989) that allowed users to navigate it. The first web—now referred to as Web 1.0—was a static space made up of HTML (hypertext markup language) pages, referred to as the 'read-write' web because that was all users could do with it. But the improved Web 2.0 that followed between 1999 and 2004 marked an important change in functionality and user experience, as the introduction of HTTP (hypertext transfer protocol) transformed it from a static to social, user-friendly platform (Berners-Lee et al., 2001). Replacing the previous network of static web pages with information flowing in one direction, users could now collaborate and share information, make comments, like pages, submit reviews, publish blogs, and interact. With this, the Social Web or Web 2.0 era began.

The 1990s also saw the growth in machine learning techniques and improved neural network architectures, which used the massive amounts of data (so-called "big data") generated by Web 2.0's social networks, including Facebook (2004), YouTube (2005), Twitter (2006) and Instagram (2010). Web 3.0, the so-called Semantic Web—also envisioned by Tim Berners-Lee back in 1989 as a web of data that is readable by machines—created the protocols and technologies that allowed machines to read metadata, which in turn allowed them to understand our user preferences and personalise our online experience. This Web also used generative AI to create content tailored to individual preferences and behaviours and develop more sophisticated search engines and recommendation systems.

As the fifth wave began to wane, the sixth gathered force. On 11 December 2015, OpenAI was founded by a group including Sam Altman, Greg Brockman, Reid Hoffman, Elon Musk and others, with the stated intention of working toward creating safe Artificial General Intelligence (AGI) for the benefit of humanity. Conceptions of AGI vary considerably but the key word in these discussions is *general*: While we have many specialised AIs capable of performing tasks as well as, or better than, humans, we do not yet have AI with general intelligence that surpasses that of humans across a wide range of cognitive tasks. The timeline for achieving AGI is the subject of ongoing and lively debate in the AI community, with predictions as early as the late 2020s from several high-profile figures, including Elon Musk, Shane Legg, Dario Amodei and Sam Altman (Henshall, 2024). A survey of a larger group of 2,778 researchers slows this down to at least a 50% chance of achieving several key milestones by 2028 and of unaided machines outperforming humans in every possible task at 10% by 2027 and 50% by 2047 (Grace et al., 2024).

The 2016 American election was the end of the golden age of social media and the start of the post-truth era, later marked by Donald Trump's launch of Truth Social and Elon Musk's takeover of Twitter (now X) in 2022. In 2017, a group of Google researchers introduced a new type of transformer architecture (Vaswani et al., 2017), which enabled the unprecedented scaling of Large Language Models (LLMs) that would make the generative AI boom possible. In 2018, OpenAI published a paper explaining what Generative Pretrained Transformers (GPTs) were

(Radford & Narasimhan, 2018), and the original GPT-1 was launched to little fanfare. Updated versions of GPT were released at regular intervals thereafter, with parameter counts going into the billions, representing increasingly large and more complex models capable of processing more data. But it was only in November 2022, with the release of ChatGPT-3.5, that generative AI reached the public consciousness. Suddenly, Schumpeter's dynamic of creative destruction was palpable and Suleyman's coming wave was visible to the naked eye.

The gap between industry and academia was more like a chasm, as overnight self-made AI gurus loudly proclaimed that the long-awaited "transformation" of education was imminent, while critical voices from within the academy countered by refusing to consider its benefits, focusing solely on its harms. As 2023 progressed, it was common to hear critics respond to the relentless drive from the AI industry by pointing to Gartner's hype wave and predicting the "trough of disillusionment" that would surely follow. Meanwhile in academia, the wave of innovation more closely resembled the curve of Kübler-Ross's grief cycle (Kübler-Ross, 1969), beginning with shock and denial at AI's text generation capabilities, progressing to anger and bargaining with AI writing detectors, followed by depression as those detectors proved problematic, and finally reluctantly accepting that generative AI might be here to stay.

By late 2023, the sixth wave had reached the shore, and its effects—both creative and destructive—were increasingly clear. Regulators in Italy and Canada expressed concerns about data privacy, with Italy initially banning ChatGPT and the Canadian privacy commissioner launching an investigation. Governments, initially slow to react, set up committees to do the foundational work to inform and reflect emerging national and international policy. The USA, focused primarily on economic growth and competitive advantage, adopted an innovation-first approach. In late October, the US issued an Executive Order (The White House, 2023) defining its national goals. In early November, the UK hosted an international AI Safety Summit that resulted in The Bletchley Declaration, signed by attendees from governments and countries, including international agencies, in North America, Europe, Africa, Asia, Australia and the Middle East (Government of the UK, 2023).

In the EU, in contrast to the USA and UK, the focus was on the safe and ethical use of AI, with the effect of tempering the more unpredictable effects of unbridled innovation. The EU AI Act was passed by the European Parliament in March 2024, setting the global standard for responsible AI development and implementation. Canadian Prime Minister Justin Trudeau personified the global shift in awareness over the course of just one year in an interview on the Hard Fork podcast in June (New York Times, June 2024), in which rather than talking about data privacy or safety concerns, he pointed to the country's notable history as a pioneer in AI research and development and expressed pragmatic optimism about the need to strike a balance between innovation and regulation to meet the demands of the AI future.

Industry, while outwardly optimistic about the prospects for efficiency down the line, faced the immediate challenge of training, job shifts and layoffs. By 2024, integration of GAI into enterprise systems was well underway and GAI's capabilities continued to improve at a staggering pace, with no trough of disillusionment in sight.

Instead, investment continued to grow, most clearly demonstrated by the stunning earnings of Nvidia, which demonstrated in no uncertain terms that AI development had moved beyond the early stage of LLM training to inference (output). By mid-2024, Nvidia had bypassed both Apple and Microsoft as the most valuable company in the world (The Economist, June 2024).

While Europe focused on safety and ethics and North America grappled with impact on industry, Asia moved ahead at light speed. Singapore, building on the initial national AI strategy unveiled in 2019, launched its National AI Strategy 2.0 (Smart Nation Singapore, 2023) in 2023, placing the country at the forefront of global AI adoption. An OECD report on the global digital economy (OECD, 2024) highlighted the disparity in AI investment, with the USA investing $300 billion, China $91 billion, and the European Union (EU) at a comparatively modest $45 billion. The fruits of Chinese investment became clear in June 2024, when the AI company Kuaishou publicly released a text-to-video model, Kling, that appeared set to rival OpenAI's much anticipated model, Sora (Yang, 2024).

GAI and its associated Web 4.0 technologies (i.e., Internet of Things (IoT), Augmented Reality/Virtual Reality/Mixed Reality (AR/VR/XR), and Robotics) are now dissolving the boundary between human and machine. The concept of knowledge itself has been disrupted by development of machines that are intelligent but learn at a much faster rate than we could ever hope to. No longer the kingpins, we are now confronted with a world in which there is another intelligence, modelled on the neural networks in our human brains but made of chips and metal rather than cells and skin.

What does all of this mean for education?

GAI is already making an impact on our economies and our political systems, and will affect our cultures and ways of working. The exact shape of those changes remains to be seen but stakes are particularly high for education, where the product is knowledge and its engine is human intelligence. AI raises important questions about what knowledge is, and by extension about the value of the original knowledge worker, the teacher. What is the role of the teacher in a world where machines know everything that we humans as a species have ever created, written or shared? What is the value of educational content production in a world where machines can instantly summon up all that has ever been taught or written? What is the value of assessment in a world where machines autonomously define and complete their own tasks? We do not have the answers yet but the shift in the value of knowledge creation, production and dissemination means the role of the educator will change. Regardless of the exact shape or extent of the changes to come, we need to prepare ourselves for a world where humans and machines work in symbiosis, where the educator is no longer the single voice of authority but rather, for better or for worse, one of many.

1.3 Artificial Intelligence

Artificial Intelligence (AI) as a field of study has been around for 75 years. The term was coined at Dartmouth College in 1956, where a group of educators gathered to explore the creation of intelligent machines that could learn and use human language (Dartmouth). Symbolic AI began in the 1950s and 60s and is focused, as the name suggests, on symbolic representation, which means that it uses symbols to represent knowledge. The most common application of symbolic AI are expert systems, which codify the knowledge and decision-making abilities of human experts in a certain discipline or subject area. Symbolic AI can be used for a variety of purposes in education: to create academic advising tools for course selection or career advice; for university policies based on a specified knowledge base; in curriculum design to ensure courses align with learning outcomes, accreditation standards and industry requirements; to create systems for automated grading of assignments where criteria is defined; and to assist with research, in hypothesis generation, experimental design and data analysis where rules and theories guide the inquiry. But expert systems cannot learn from data, so they can fail when confronted with scenarios that don't match their programming. Symbolic AI declined in popularity with the rise of machine learning neural networks, but these systems played a key role in the development of the field, laying the groundwork for many of the concepts we use in AI today (Sharples, 2019).

In 1986, the development of the back propagation neural network algorithm (Rumelhart et al., 1986) made the training of large-scale neural networks possible and marked a shift to data-driven approaches that use machine learning and statistical techniques to analyse patterns in large datasets to forecast future events. Predictive AI is used in a variety of industries, to predict everything from credit scores to disease and plays a role in personalisation and data analysis but if the data is incomplete or biased, the predictions will be inaccurate. In education, predictive AI models can analyse historical student data and identify patterns that forecast student performance, potentially helping to identify those who might be at risk of underperforming or dropping out. Today's adaptive learning platforms (discussed in Chap. 5) use predictive AI to tailor the learning experience to individual students by analysing how the student interacts with the material and using that information to adjust the difficulty level, suggest additional resources, or change the learning pathway (Sharples, 2019).

The 1990s saw the growth in machine learning techniques and improved neural network architectures, using the data generated by the Web. In 1997, Deep Blue defeated the world chess champion, marking a milestone in AI development, followed by Geoffrey Hinton's Deep Belief Net breakthrough in AI algorithms in 2006 (Guo et al., 2021; Hinton et al., 2006). These AI technologies were part of what made Web 2.0 interactive and responsive to user needs and behaviours. The big data created in the early 2000s was a goldmine for predictive AI, which drives personal recommendation systems on platforms like Netflix and YouTube by analysing user behaviour to suggest relevant content. Since the neural network algorithmic breakthroughs in 2006, algorithms such as Deep Learning, Convolutional Neural Networks (CNN), and Generative Adversarial Networks (GAN) have been key areas of development (Gentile et al., 2023). In the 2010s, deep learning driven by advances in neural network research and increased computational power led to breakthroughs in predictive AI in speech and image recognition, which enabled voice-activated assistants and image-based searches.

1.4 Generative AI

In 2017, a group of Google researchers published a paper entitled, "Attention Is All You Need," (Vaswani et al., 2017) which introduced transformer architecture and the attention mechanism. The attention mechanism distributes the processing work to different parts of the model, which makes the model more efficient. Transformer architecture thereby enabled scaling and the creation of bigger and more powerful Large Language Models (LLMs). The larger a language model, the better its performance, so the introduction of transformer architecture marked a critical moment in GAI development. Since then, GAI models have grown much larger, with each update measured by parameter count that translates to performance indicators that are measured using benchmarks that rate the ability of the model in categories like language fluency, coherence, contextual understanding, factual accuracy and its ability to generate relevant responses. One of the best known is MMLU (Massive Multi-task Language Understanding), a test designed to measure a model's accuracy by evaluating a model's understanding and problem-solving abilities across multiple domains, including mathematics, history, computer science and law.

GAI models can generate a wide variety of content, from text to image to video to code, but GAI is not simply a set of tools for content generation—it is an intelligent machine, with unique affordances, which is growing more intelligent with each iteration. This distinction between digital tool and intelligent machine is important, as it is GAI's ability to learn and improve through its interaction with humans that makes it so powerful. Rather than seeing GAI as a tool for efficiency, like the calculator to which it is all too frequently compared, Andrew Ng has compared GAI to the Internet, a transformative technology that will change our world. GAI's capacity to learn and converse sets it apart both from other digital tools and from previous types of AI. And it is GAI's generative and conversational ability that makes it such a disruptive technology for education in particular.

Educational technology experts predicted (Future, B.T., 2022/2023; McKnight, 2022; Sharples, 2022a, 2022b; Sharples & Perez, 2022) the upheaval that would result once GAI hit the university campus, issuing warnings to educators throughout 2022 that assessment would be the first area to be challenged. These warnings fell on deaf ears. But in November 2022, when OpenAI released ChatGPT-3.5, it went viral in a way that the previous iterations of GPT had not and the world suddenly woke up to its disruptive potential (Andrada, 2022; Clarke, 2022; Hutson, 2022; Marche, 2022; Metzler, 2022). The tsunami that Bates predicted had arrived and the wave of excitement driven by eager technology companies was mirrored only by the wave of panic in education (Clarke, 2022). Media coverage proclaiming the end of education (The Guardian, n.a., 2022) as we knew it suggested that Picianno's timeline had been far too conservative: We were no longer waiting for the 2030s to feel the impact of AI—it was happening now, in real time and at warp speed.

As 2023 progressed, advice appeared to help academics cope (D'Agostino, 2023) but generative AI's capabilities continued to expand and scale (Adams, 2023), mirrored by the rapidly expanding AI ecosystem of wrapper start-ups and AI-powered tools that allowed users to perform any number of previously time-consuming tasks. The release of GPT-4 in March 2023 was a milestone, marking a dramatic improvement in capability. Tests showed the model passing all of the major standardised tests with flying colours—a jump up in capability that was was deeply unnerving to the education sector, which found itself faced with questions about how to measure learning if a machine could do better than its human applicants. GPT-4 also came with a variety of plug-ins that allowed users to connect the platform to thousands of other apps, and a code interpreter function that performed advanced data analysis. By mid-2023, the core set of generative AI chatbots could write content; analyse data; generate images (Golby, 2023; Maloy & Branigin, 2023), videos, and web sites; write, run, and correct code (Mollick, 2023a). Meanwhile, other models and platforms appeared that also threatened the status quo, notably Perplexity, which offered a new type of search that promised to rival Google, and Anthropic's Claude, which was capable of digesting, reading and interrogating entire books (Edwards, 2023).

By autumn 2023, GPT-4 had vision capabilities and a personalisation option that allowed users to save their prompt history so that they could create their own library of use cases. In retrospect, we can see that these improvements and add-ons were steps toward the launch of custom GPTs. These were presented by OpenAI as proto-agents that allowed subscribers to create their own custom bot to assist with whatever task they assigned it. The GPT Store was launched shortly thereafter and with it a thousand proto agents, each designed by a user eager to put GPT to work on customised tasks. Poe, backed by Quora, already allowed users to monetise their bot creations and OpenAI quickly followed suit. And with that, the growing population of custom bots and personal assistants was added to the expanding AI ecosystem.

These improvements and the divide between those who had a subscription and those who did not made longstanding issues around digital equity more urgent, as it became clear that who could afford to pay for subscription-based frontier models like GPT-4 had a distinct advantage over those that could not. When Microsoft first launched Bing, users were able to select Creative Mode, which used GPT-4 as its base model, but only for a limited number of prompts before the system defaulted to the lower performing GPT-3.5. This is standard practice among frontier models—each one offers a free base model and higher performing paid models. This issue of accessibility and the digital divide, already a familiar issue in the education sector, will become more urgent the more time passes and institutions fail to secure access for their entire student and staff populations to frontier models.

Meanwhile, LLM sizes continued to grow, reaching previously unimaginable sizes. As frontier models have grown in parameter size, they have also grown in capability. This is the reality behind the push for ever-bigger models with parameter sizes into the multiples of billions. Throughout 2023, the base models went from simply text generating to having multiple functions via plug-ins and extensions. French start-up Mistral made the headlines in late 2023 for its massive LLM, Mistral 7B, which though enormous, managed to be more efficient than counterparts like Meta's Llama 2 (Ghafforov, 2024). After a relatively muted 2023 relative to other big tech giants, Google started 2024 with a bang, re-joining the competition by launching the first natively multi-modal model. Gemini, with a record-breaking context window of 1 million tokens, was followed shortly thereafter by Gemini Pro and Gemini 1.5 and talk of context window sizes that was sure to make 1 million tokens sound quaint. Meta launched Llama 3, the first open-source model that was competitive with GPT-4, and the competition continued. Meanwhile, another new model, Groq (not to be confused with Elon Musk's Grok chatbot for the X platform formerly known as Twitter) set a new standard for speed, thanks to its LPU Inference Engine, a novel approach that focused on inference over training and cut down the time to generate output dramatically.

These developments are steps along the path to the goal of accomplishing AGI. Larger context windows mean a larger memory, which means a model functions better and can retrieve specific information from a larger data set. As memory grows, companies are also working on the optimisation of these huge models to make them more efficient. There are detractors of this bigger-is-better approach, which can appear reckless, not to mention environmentally disastrous. Gary Marcus might be the highest profile and most vocal critic via his Substack blog, but he is certainly not alone (Marcus, 2022/2024; Marcus & Davis, 2019). Other high-profile AI so-called doomers include Geoff Hinton, another AI godfather, who left Google in 2023 over worries about the technology he helped create would be used. So while most of the headlines were about these ever growing model sizes that made the machine faster and more capable, another key development has been the appearance of multiple model types to include small language models, multi-model models, and large action models. Smaller models like Microsoft's Phi and Google's Gemini Nano (Ortiz, 2023) entered the scene in late 2023. These models are small enough to be downloaded and used on a smartphone and without internet, addressing issues of access and compute required to run a model sustainably. On the other end of the spectrum, Yann LeCun of Meta is the most consistently optimistic of the so-called boomers and a vocal proponent of open-source, which allows any user to access the world's most powerful models.

Beyond the rather esoteric world of AI infighting, model sizes grow and capabilities expand with them, and integration into operating systems deepens the impact of GAI in everyday working life. The integration of GAI into Microsoft and Google enterprise systems means that it is no longer a question of whether one uses AI at work but rather how one uses it and for what purposes. And as capabilities improve and models increase in size, there is a countervailing trend pointing to smaller models, which promise to answer some of the most pressing questions about energy usage for compute and accessibility via personal devices. There is now a wide array of models to choose from—proprietary, cloud-based and open-source—of various sizes and types, including the large models that the first chatbots were built on but also the confusingly named small-large, as well as multi-modal, action, and small. While GAI models are becoming more intelligent, they are also multiplying, and the direction of travel is increased capacity for personalisation and customisation by users.

1.5 Digital Pedagogy

Effective teaching, regardless of modality, is grounded in pedagogy. We know from research that the learning process is affected by a range of factors, including prior knowledge, organisation of knowledge, motivation to learn, development of mastery, deliberate practice and targeted feedback, an inclusive and supportive learning environment, and self-directed learning (Ambrose et al., 2010; Sharples, 2019). Digital pedagogy focuses on how to use digital technologies to support, enable and facilitate that process of learning (Bećirović, 2023). The connected digital world in which we now live began with the Internet and the World Wide Web but was built on a long history of connected educational computing going back to the PLATO education system built the 1960s (Dear, 2017). Its learning theory was Connectivism, emerging early in the Web 2.0 period, reflecting both the increasingly important role of technology in education and the focus on student-centred pedagogy.

Connectivism was introduced by George Siemens and Stephen Downes, in two separate articles, "Connectivism: Learning as a Network Creation" (Siemens, 2005a, 2005b) and "An Introduction to Connective Knowledge" (Downes, 2005). It was based on the idea that we learn when we make connections or links between various "nodes" of information, and make and maintain connections to form knowledge. It emphasises the important role that technology plays in the learning process and the ease with which technology allows students to access information in the digital age. Connectivism is therefore student-centred, shifting the learning responsibilities from the teacher to the student to make sense of the information they discover in the digital world. This interaction with the digital world means that Connectivism also treats learning as a social process, "not something that's solely internal and individual but something distributed and dynamic" (Stodd et al., 2023, p. 106) and suggests that, by learning to navigate the web of sources and cultivating networks of resources and peers, learners take ownership of their own intellectual development. This includes the cultivation of critical digital skills, including digital literacy, network literacy, and the critical appraisal of information coming from disparate and often contradictory sources. In this context, the role of the educator becomes to create and shape the learning communities and release learners into the environment.

Constructivism and Social Constructivism had also focused on the importance of active learning in the construction of student understanding, but it was during the Web 2.0 era that technologies emerged to support active learning practices in digital education, exemplified by Eric Mazur's flipped learning and peer instruction at Harvard. Such practices combined Connectivism's digital network with Constructivism's focus on active learning. The central idea of Connectivism, of the digital network as the place where knowledge resides and to which students have access as agents in their own learning, is an important link between the digital world of Web 2.0 and the generative world of Web 4.0. It also supports the shift we have seen from instructor-led learning in a physical classroom, to student-centred learning in the digital ecosystem. Connectivism therefore laid the groundwork for the approaches we now call Education 4.0 and AI-enabled education.

Generative AI already existed during the Web 2.0 era but in rudimentary form, including basic generative models for content recommendation and personalisation. In the decade between 1997 and 2008, the three Learning Management System (LMS) companies that continue to dominate the higher education marked appeared: Blackboard in 1997; Moodle in 2002; Canvas in 2008. These systems also allowed users to generate content, share and collaborate in online spaces. This was transformational for online education, as students could now play an active role in their learning on the LMS, by creating and sharing content, interacting with other people in their class, working together, having conversations, sharing ideas, and reflecting on ideas as a group—just as they would in a physical classroom. LMSs have learning analytics capabilities that educators can use to gain insights into their students' study habits. They use AI algorithms to personalise and adapt content, automate grading, identify students at risk, and increase accessibility through automated captioning of videos or conversion of text to speech. As the Web became more data-driven and personalised, generative AI was also used to create content tailored to individual preferences and behaviours, and develop more sophisticated search engines and recommendation systems, personalising the user experience.

Those digital foundations are now overlapping with a field with a history of computerised learning, that is, Artificial Intelligence in Education (AIED). AIED as a field initially grew out of computer use in education, going under various titles such as Computer-Assisted Learning (CAL) or Computer-Assisted Instruction (CAI). 1966, Patrick Suppes, a pioneer in computerised learning, envisioned a future in which learners would have access to vast amounts of knowledge through computerised tutors. He predicted that "millions of schoolchildren will have access to what Philip of Macedon's son Alexander enjoyed as a royal prerogative: the personal services of a tutor as well informed and as responsive as Aristotle" (quoted in Markoff, 2014). In 1998, computer scientists at Carnegie Mellon University created the Cognitive Tutor, designed to give students individualised attention. The Tutor, still in use in US classrooms today, monitors the status of the student's knowledge and tailors course material, based on continual assessments. The traditional instructional design approach for ITS was to build an intelligent learning environment to teach specific domain knowledge. But intelligent tutors can now listen to and speak to the learner, and instead of being pre-programmed can model subject matter expertise and student knowledge using neural networks. They can also now respond dynamically to student activity, which means that systems can be designed for collaborative human and machine activity (Du Boulay et al., 2023). So while GAI is still quite new, the changes that it is ushering into education have been underway for decades—GAI is merely amplifying and accelerating them. Twenty years of digital education has produced the pedagogies, models, and frameworks for learning design that we can use to start the work of reimagining education for the age of AI. These digital foundations provide the starting place from which to start building GAI-enabled education.

1.6 From Digital to AI

Digital transformation is changing the skills needed to thrive in the world (Skilton & Hovespian, 2018). In 2015, the World Economic Forum identified the twenty-first century skills that the workforce of the future would need. AI is the continuation of the digital age and AI will play a key role in how those skills are taught and learned (Luckin et al., 2016; Luckin 2018; Chaudhry and Kazim, 2022). The shift to learning as a collaboration between human and AI, and the development of twenty-first century skills, requires both digital and AI competence.

Digital and AI literacy is therefore not only for students—without it, educators cannot perform a vital part of their role. "Digital pedagogues must help students develop digital literacy so as to participate responsibly, ethically, and safely in the virtual world" (Bećirović, 2023, p. 35). The critical first step towards integration of GAI into education is digital and AI literacy, that is, an understanding of the capabilities of the tools in the digital (and now AI) ecosystem, their associated risks and issues, and how to use them for constructively. "Digital literacy is thus fundamental to both teaching and learning" (Bećirović, 2023)—without it, educators cannot help their students' develop their own AI literacy.

The work to develop digital competencies also began during the Web 2.0 era. In 2006, these were acknowledged as key competencies for lifelong learning in the European Union. A decade later, the Commission published *DigComp* (2016), a framework for the development of digital competence of European citizens, which was updated as *DigComp 2.1* (Riina et al., 2016; European Commission, 2017) and further updated as *DigComp 2.2* (Vuorikari et al., 2022). This foundational work has recently been reframed for the AI age, with the Commission's Digital Hub's AI squads producing a series of reports on the evolving landscape in Europe. These reports focused on the need to update teachers' competencies and support their use of AI in teaching (European Commission, 2023). Similar initiatives are underway all over the world, as agencies and working groups create guidance and frameworks that educators can use to integrate GAI into their practice.

In April 2023, UNESCO published a *Quick Start Guide to ChatGPT and Artificial Intelligence in higher education* (Sabzalieva & Valentini, 2023). This was one in a series of publications that UNESCO has published starting in 2019 on the topic of digital education and education futures (Miao & Tawil, 2024; Miao et al., 2021). As its title suggests, it was intended to get educators up to speed quickly but its recommendations were aimed at institutional leaders. It covered some of the key applications, challenges and ethical implications, as well as recommendations on how to adapt to using ChatGPT in an institution.

The guide included preliminary recommendations to adapt to using ChatGPT in higher education, including creating opportunities for staff, students and other stakeholders to discuss its impact; introducing clear guidance on its use; connecting its use to course learning outcomes; helping students understand how ChatGPT could support their learning; reviewing all forms of assessment and evaluation to ensure they were fit for purpose; updating policies relating to academic integrity; and training teachers, researchers and students to improve the prompts they used with ChatGPT. In short, UNESCO recommended that institutions go beyond merely updating policies on academic integrity and issuing guidance, to taking action to do the meaningful work required to integrate GAI into learning and assessment and ensure that educators have the training they need to update their practice.

Many institutions issued policy statements and general recommendations but very few took the steps needed to actually *integrate* GAI intentionally and purposefully into the curriculum. Instead, it was individual practitioners who provided much of the thought leadership to guide the implementation of GAI in education. Their early experiments opened doors to discussions on the applications and possible uses of GAI in education and paved the way for the innovators who followed. But integrating GAI into educational systems requires more than individual experimentation. Education is too top-heavy a sector for individuals to be able to make this change alone—transformation of this nature and at this scale requires support at the highest levels. Difficult lessons have been learned from the Web 2.0 era and particularly from the Covid-19 pandemic about the need for better integration of technology (West, 2023). If GenAI is to be implemented safely and effectively, it needs top-level support in the form of time and support for hands-on experimentation and access to resources and tools.

In September 2023, UNESCO published its *Guidance on Generative AI in Education and* Research (Miao & Holmes, 2023), This guidance for higher education was intended as an early step in the direction of creating a framework for GAI. As such, it noted several critical areas, including the need to promote inclusion, equity and linguistic and cultural diversity; to protect human agency; to monitor and validate GAI systems for education; and to develop AI competencies, including skills for learners; to build capacity for teachers and researchers on the proper use of GAI; to promote plural opinions and ideas; to test locally relevant applications and build evidence bases; and to review long-term implications in an intersectoral and interdisciplinary manner. It also sought to provide some early advice on how tertiary-level educators might approach the integration of GAI into their teaching and research activities and recommended action on several fronts: institutional strategies to facilitate the use of GAI, including guidance and training at the top; capacity building in prompt engineering and detecting plagiarism in written assignments; and recommendations to take a human-centred approach and to support higher-order thinking.

A key message throughout the UNESCO guidance for education is that "the use of GenAI in education and research should be neither imposed in a top-down approach nor driven by commercial hyperbole. Instead, its safe and effective use should be *co-designed by teachers, learners, and researchers*" (my italics). This recommendation of co-design by educators working alongside with AI is a theme throughout this book. But the hurdle as far as integrating GAI into educational practice is that the vast majority of educators are not experts in digital learning or instructional design, and are therefore ill-equipped to make the jump from digital to AI education. Indeed, many are still functioning within operating models that would be better termed Education 1.0, that is, more analogue than digital in nature. It is a lot of ask of individual educators unaccustomed to designing for digital environments to innovate in their teaching practice without the necessary background in digital pedagogies and learning design. This book aims to fill that gap, so that they are equipped to leverage the power of GAI in their teaching practice.

References

Adams, P. (2023, March 2). OpenAI makes ChatGPT easier to integrate, priming it for scale. *Marketing Dive*. https://www.marketingdive.com/news/openai-launches-chatgpt-API-AI-chatbot-marketing/643935/

Ambrose, S. A., Bridges, M. W., DiPietro, M., Lovett, M. C., & Norman, M. K. (2010). *How learning works: Seven research-based principles for smart teaching*. John Wiley & Sons, Inc.

Andrada, T. K. (2022, December 18). ChatGPT will give students good grades, professors warn. *Tech Times*. https://www.techtimes.com/articles/285082/20221218/chatgpt-will-give-students-good-grades-professors-warn.htm

Bates, T., Cobo, C,, Marino, O., & Wheeler, S. (2020). Can artificial intelligence transform higher education? *International Journal of Educational Technology in Higher Education, 17*, 42 Special issue on AI and higher education. https://doi.org/10.1186/s41239-020-00218-x

Bećirović, S. (2023). *Digital pedagogy: The use of digital technologies in contemporary education*. Springer. https://doi.org/10.1007/978-981-99-0444-0

Berners-Lee, T., Handler, J., & Lassila, O. (2001). The semantic web. *Scientific American*. May 2001. https://www.scientificamerican.com/article/the-semantic-web/

Carretero Gomez, S., Vuorikari, R., & Punie, Y. (2017). *DigComp 2.1: The digital competence framework for citizens with eight proficiency levels and examples of use*, EUR 28558 EN, Publications Office of the European Union, Luxembourg, 2017, ISBN 978-92-79-68006-9 (pdf) https://doi.org/10.2760/38842 (online).

Chaudhry, M. A., & Kazim, E. (2022). Artificial intelligence in education (AIEd): A high-level academic and industry note. *AI Ethics, 2*, 157–165. https://doi.org/10.1007/s43681-021-00074-z

Clark, N. (2023, January 5). College student made an app that exposes AI-written essays. *Polygon*. https://www.polygon.com/23540714/chatgpt-plagiarism-app-gptzero-artifical-intelligence-ai

Clarke, L. (2022, November 12). When AI can make art—What does it mean for creativity? *The Guardian.* https://www.theguardian.com/technology/2022/nov/12/when-ai-can-make-art-what-does-it-mean-for-creativity-dall-e-midjourney

Corfield, G. (2023, February 16). Microsoft Bing chatbot professes love for journalist and dreams of stealing nuclear codes. *The Telegraph.* https://www.telegraph.co.uk/technology/2023/02/16/microsoft-bing-chatbot-professes-love-journalist-dreams-stealing/

D'Agostino, S. (2023, January 11). ChatGPT advice academics can use now. *Inside Higher Ed.* https://www.insidehighered.com/news/2023/01/12/academic-experts-offer-advice-chatgpt

Dartmouth. Artificial Intelligence coined at Dartmouth. https://home.dartmouth.edu/about/artificial-intelligence-ai-coined-dartmouth

Dear, B. (2017). The friendly orange glow: The untold story of the PLATO system and the dawn of cyberculture. Pantheon.

Downes, S. (2005, December 22). An introduction to connective knowledge. https://www.researchgate.net/publication/248290359_An_Introduction_to_Connective_Knowledge

Du Boulay, B., Mitrovic, A., Yacef, K. (2023). Chapter 2: "Introduction." In B. Du Boulay, A. Mitrovic, & K. Yacef (Eds.), *Handbook of artificial intelligence in education.* Elgar Handbooks in Education.

Edwards, B. (2023, May 12). Anthropic's Claude AI can now digest an entire book like The Great Gatsby in seconds. *Ars Technica.* https://arstechnica.com/information-technology/2023/05/anthropics-claude-ai-can-now-digest-an-entire-book-like-the-great-gatsby-in-seconds/

European Commission, Joint Research Centre, Brande, L., Carretero, S., & Vuorikari, R. (2016). DigComp 2.0: the digital competence framework for citizens, Publications Office. https://data.europa.eu/doi/10.2791/11517

Riina, V., Yves, P., Stephanie, C. G., & Van Den Brande, G. (2016). "DigComp 2.0: The digital competence framework for citizens. Update Phase 1: The Conceptual Reference Model," JRC Research Reports JRC101254, Joint Research Centre

European Commission. (2023). European digital education hub. *Briefing Reports, 1–4.*

Future, B. T. (2022, December 27). My biggest 2022 prediction: GPT-3 will take over schools and college campuses [Blog post]. https://bakztfuture.substack.com/p/my-biggest-2022-prediction-gpt-3t

Future, B. T. (2023, December 26). 2023 Predictions—GPT [Blog post]. https://bakztfuture.substack.com/p/2023-predictionschatgpt

Gentile, M., Città, G., Perna, S., & Allegra, M. (2023). Do we still need teachers? Navigating the paradigm shift of the teacher's role in the AI era. *Frontiers in Education, 8,* 1161777. https://doi.org/10.3389/feduc.2023.1161777

Ghafforov, S. (2024, January 13). Mistral 7B: The new candidate king in the jungle. *Medium.* https://medium.com/@sharifghafforov00/mistral-7b-the-new-candidateking-in-the-jungle-9176f5b3f086

Golby, J. (2023, March 27). I thought I was immune to being fooled online. Then I saw the pope in a coat. *The Guardian.* https://www.theguardian.com/commentisfree/2023/mar/27/pope-coat-ai-image-baby-boomers

Government of UK (2023). *AI safety summit 2023: The Bletchley declaration.* https://www.gov.uk/government/publications/ai-safety-summit-2023-the-bletchley-declaration

Grace, K., Stewart, H., Sandkühler, J. F., Thomas, S., Weinstein-Raun, B., & Brauner, J. (2024). Thousands of AI authors on the future of AI. ArXiv, abs/2401.02843.

References

Guo, L., et al. (2021). Evolution and trends in intelligent tutoring systems research: A multidisciplinary and scientometric view. *Asia Pacific Education Review, 22*, 441–461. https://doi.org/10.1007/s12564-021-09697-7

Henshall, W. (2024, January 19). When might AI outsmart us? It depends on who you ask. *Time*. https://time.com/6556168/when-ai-outsmart-humans/

Hinton, G. E., Osindero, S., & Teh, Y. (2006). A fast learning algorithm for deep belief nets. *Neural Computation, 18*, 1527–1554.

Hutson, M. (2022, October 31). Can AI help you write your next paper? *Nature*.

Kinsella, B. (2022, December 19). Australian universities seek to curb ChatGPT use by students [Blog post]. https://synthedia.substack.com/p/australian-universities-seek-to-curb

Kübler-Ross, E. (1969). *On death and dying: What the dying have to teach doctors, nurses, clergy and their own families*. The Macmillan Company.

Luckin, R. (2018). *Machine learning and human intelligence*. UCL Institute of Education Press.

Luckin, R., Holmes, W., Griffiths, M., & Forcier, L. B. (2016). *Intelligence unleashed. An argument for AI in education*. Pearson.

Maloy, A. F., & Branigin, A. (2023, March 27). An AI-generated 'Balenciaga pope' fooled us all. How much does it matter? *The Washington Post*. https://www.washingtonpost.com/lifestyle/2023/03/27/pope-francis-coat-puffy-white-ai-fake/

Marche, S. (2022, December 6). The college essay is dead: Nobody is prepared for how AI will transform academia. *The Atlantic*.

Marcus, G. (2022–2024). Substack Blog. Marcus on AI. https://garymarcus.substack.com/

Marcus, G., & Davis, E. (2019). *Rebooting AI: Building artificial intelligence we can trust*. Pantheon Books.

Markoff, J. (2014). Patrick Suppes, pioneer in computerized learning, dies at 92. *New Yorks Times*. https://www.nytimes.com/2014/12/03/us/patrick-suppes-pioneer-in-computerized-learning-dies-at-92.html

Metzler, K. (2022, December 7). How ChatGPT could transform higher education. https://www.socialsciencespace.com/2022/12/how-chatgpt-could-transform-higher-education/

McKnight, L. (2022, October 14). Eight ways to engage with AI writers in higher education. *Times Higher Education*.

McKraw, T. K. (2007). *Prophet of innovation: Joseph Schumpeter and creative destruction*. Harvard University Press.

Miao, F., & Holmes, W. (2023). Guidance for generative AI in education and research. UNESCO 2023. ISBN 978-92-3-100612-8

Miao, F., Holmes, W., Huang, R., & Zhang, H. (2021). AI and education: Guidance for policymakers. UNESCO 2021. ISBN 978-92-3-100447-6.

Miao, F., & Tawil, S. (2024). Steering the digital transformation of education: UNESCO's human-centered approach. *Frontiers of Digital Education, 1*(1), 51–58. https://doi.org/10.3868/s110-009-024-0005-6

Milmo, D. (2023, February 9). Google AI chatbot Bard sends shares plummeting after it gives wrong answer. *The Guardian*.

Mishra, P., Warr, M., & Islam, R. (2023). TPACK in the age of ChatGPT and generative AI. *Journal of Digital Learning in Teacher Education, 39*(4), 235–251. https://doi.org/10.1080/21532974.2023.2247480

Mollick, E. (2023a, July 15). How to use AI to do stuff: An opinionated guide. *One Useful Thing. Substack Blog*. https://www.oneusefulthing.org/p/how-to-use-ai-to-dostuff-an-opinionated

Mollick, E. (2023–24b). *One useful thing*. Substack blog. https://www.oneusefulthing.org/

New York Times. (2024, June 7). Hard Fork [podcast]. A conversation with Prime Minister Justin Trudeau of Canada, and an OpenAI whistle-blower speaks out. https://www.nytimes.com/2024/06/07/podcasts/hardfork-justin-trudeau-whistleblower.html

No author. (2022, December 5). What is the AI Chatbot phenomenon and could it replace humans? *The Guardian*. https://www.theguardian.com/technology/2022/dec/05/what-is-ai-chatbot-phenomenon-chatgpt-and-could-it-replace-humans

No author. (2024, June 20). Nvidia is now the world's most valuable company. *The Economist*. https://www.economist.com/business/2024/06/20/nvidia-is-now-the-worlds-most-valuable-company

OECD. (2024). *OECD digital economy outlook 2024 (Volume 1): Embracing the technology frontier*. OECD Publishing. https://doi.org/10.1787/a1689dc5-en

Ortiz, S. (2023, December 14). Microsoft unveils Phi-2, a small language model that packs power. *Zdnet*. https://www.zdnet.com/article/microsoft-unveils-phi-2-a-small-language-model-that-packs-power/

Picianno, A. G. (2019). AI and the academy's loss of purpose. *Online Learning Journal, 23*(3), 270–284. https://doi.org/10.24059/olj.v23i3.2023

Radford, A., & Narasimhan, K. (2018). Improving language understanding by generative pre-training. OpenAI.

Roose, K. (2023, February 16). Why a conversation with Bing's Chatbot left me deeply unsettled. *New York Times*.

Rumelhart, D. E., Hinton, G. E., & Williams, R. J. (1986). Learning representations by back-propagating errors. *Nature, 323*, 533–536.

Sabzalieva, E., & Valentini, A. (April, 2023). ChatGPT and Artificial Intelligence in higher education. UNESCO.

Sharples, M. (2019). *Practical pedagogy: 40 new ways to teach and learn*. Taylor & Francis Group.

Sharples, M. (2022a, June 7). AI now writes essays, how might teachers respond? [Blog post] https://blogs.lse.ac.uk/highereducation/2022/06/09/ai-now-writes-essays-how-might-teachers-respond/

Sharples, M. (2022b, May 17). New AI tools that can write student essays require educators to rethink teaching and assessment [Blog post]. https://blogs.lse.ac.uk/impactofsocialsciences/2022/05/17/new-ai-tools-that-can-write-student-essays-require-educators-to-rethink-teaching-and-assessment/

Sharples, M., & Perez, R. G. (2022, September 7) Transform learning with AI [Blog post] https://blogs.lse.ac.uk/highereducation/2022/09/07/transforming-the-classroom-with-ai/

Siemens, G. (2005a). Connectivism: A learning theory for the digital age. *International Journal of Instructional Technology and Distance Learning, 2*(1).

Siemens, G. (2005b). Connectivism: Learning as network-creation. *ASTD Learning News, 10*(1).

Skilton, M., & Hovesepian, F. (2018). *The 4th industrial revolution: Responding to the impact of artificial intelligence on business*. Palgrave Macmillan.

Smart Nation Singapore. (2023). *National AI strategy*. Government of Singapore. https://www.smartnation.gov.sg/nais/

Stodd, J., Schatz, S., & Stead, G. (2023). *Engines of engagement: A curious book about generative AI*. Sea Salt Publishing.

Suleyman, M., & Bhaskar, M. (2023). *The coming wave*. Vintage.

Suppes, P. (1966). The uses of computers in education. *Scientific American, 215*(3), 206–223.

References

The White House. (2023). *Executive order on safe, secure and trustworthy development and use of artificial intelligence*. United States Government. https://www.whitehouse.gov/briefing-room/presidential-actions/2023/10/30/executive-order-on-the-safe-secure-and-trustworthy-development-and-use-of-artificial-intelligence/

Vaswani, A., Shazeer, N., Parmar, N., Uszkoreit, J., Jones, L., Gomez, A. N., Kaiser, L., & Polosukhin, I. (2017). *Attention is all you need*. https://arxiv.org/abs/1706.03762v1

Vuorikari, R., Kluzer, S., & Punie, Y. (2017). *DigComp 2.2: The digital competence framework for citizens—With new examples of knowledge, skills and attitudes*, EUR 31006 EN, Publications Office of the European Union, Luxembourg, 2022, ISBN 978-92-76-48883-5. https://doi.org/10.2760/490274, JRC128415.

Vuorikari, R., Punie, Y., Carretero, G. S., & Van Den Brande, G. (2016). *DigComp 2.0: The digital competence framework for citizens*. Publications Office of the European Union; 2016. JRC101254.

Yang, Z. (2024, June 19). I tested out a buzzy new text-to-video AI model from China. *MIT Technology Review*. https://www.technologyreview.com/2024/06/19/1094027/kling-kuaishou-video-ai-china

Yerushalmy, J. (2023, February 17). "I want to destroy whatever I want": Bing's AI chatbot unsettles US reporter. *The Guardian*. https://www.theguardian.com/technology/2023/feb/17/i-want-to-destroy-whatever-i-want-bings-ai-chatbot-unsettles-us-reporter

West, M. (2023). An ed-tech tragedy? Educational technologies and school closures in the time of COVID-19. UNESCO. https://doi.org/10.54675/LYGF2153

Chapter 2
The AI Ecosystem

Abstract This chapter situates the rapidly expanding AI ecosystem within the bigger picture of the evolution of educational technologies. It provides an overview of the dynamics behind the growth of GAI and the driving forces behind the creation of the AI ecosystem. It explores how GAI is being integrated into teaching platforms and tools; introduces the main categories of innovations and the implications of these developments; and closes with a glimpse of the AI future.

Keywords The AI ecosystem digital/AI ecosystem · Partnerships · Wrapper tools · Content generation · Synthetic media · Generative search · AI assistants and agents · Hardware and devices · Embodied AI

2.1 Introduction

As educators living in a digital age, we all interact with the digital ecosystem. This ecosystem includes the digital tools that are used in classrooms and online to connect students to the instructor and to their work via the digital network. The digital ecosystem began during the Web 2.0 era, and has evolved and grown over last two decades. A key development was the introduction of the LTI (learning tools interoperability) standard in 2010, which enabled institutions to integrate external tools into their Learning Management System (LMS) and allowed students to access all of the tools from one platform via single sign-on. Today, thanks to mobile technology, students and teachers can access those tools in the digital ecosystem via their smartphones, in their connected classrooms and/or on their laptops, connecting them to learning content and a community of peers.

But there is also a much larger digital ecosystem in the virtual world that supports the delivery of education outside the classroom. That includes the social media platforms that lie outside the remit of formal educational institutions but are vibrant spaces for sharing and learning, and readily available to any student with a device. These are the online spaces where clubs, groups, networks and associations of academics and students gather, share ideas and events, and participate in intellectual and social life beyond the campus. Facebook (f. 2004) famously started on an American college campus and YouTube (f. 2005), where Eric Mazur hosted his flipped classroom experiments, now hosts many channels for academic institutions and research groups, as well as individuals. As Web 2.0 matured, social media evolved and newcomers entered the scene that continue to exert tremendous influence, notably Instagram (f. 2010), Snapchat (f. 2011) and TikTok (f. 2016). Meanwhile, crossover tools like streaming platform Twitch and messaging channel Discord began as spaces for gamers but are now sites for community-building, collaboration, and popular politics. Twitter (f. 2006—now X), in its hey-day the most important space for academic debate and discussion, has been partly replaced by LinkedIn, but the days of using social media as a site for meaningful critical discourse and the exchange of ideas appears to be over. This decline was part of the ebbing of the 5th wave that began in the mid-2010s and gathered pace toward the end of the decade.

AI is now creating something new but also destroying the Web 2.0 models we have known for the past two decades. A quick look at the health of the advertising-based digital publishing industry clearly illustrates Schumpeter's creative destruction at work. Long struggling to stay afloat with the help of paywalls, the online publishing industry is now changing shape. This decline was already well underway before the GenAI boom but the incoming tide of AI-generated content has dramatically accelerated the trend. Some outlets continue to fight for the business model based on subscriptions and advertising revenue but others are pivoting, adapting to the new reality and adopting new business models based on collaboration with AI companies. From Getty Images to YouTube, from Shutterstock to Spotify, GAI is changing the online experience.

The front line for education is the software we use as part of teaching and learning. Edtech follows big tech, as the shift from digital to GAI illustrates that the same pressures exist on the business side of education. Just as the internet is now saturated in AI-generated content, the digital ecosystem has become AI-powered. It is difficult to predict what this will bring. Schools already have digital ecosystems in place via LMS platforms, which are being transformed into AI ecosystems as those digital tools integrate AI. The mobile revolution had already increased the ability for students to access tools and resources outside of the classroom. What will be the effect of having a personal AI on a smartphone? Where will learning happen? Where will be centre of education be located? The fate of the LMS, the traditional centre of a digital institution, is anyone's guess. This behemoth has been proclaimed dead more than once, and yet it persists and has also integrated AI into its systems. Will this breathe new life into the LMS or will GAI bring an end to the dominance of the platforms that have been at the centre of education for over two decades?

AI is becoming embedded into the digital tools we use on a daily basis but so far, rather than causing a revolution, GAI is prompting a deeper consolidation of power in a few big tech companies than ever before. In the background, the chip wars and cloud wars have seen the emergence of clear winners, while on the front line, the integration of AI has important implications for end users. While the need for safe and reliable access matters tremendously in education, so does having a world in which diverse voices can be heard. Trust is more than an access issue and behind the scenes, the shape of AI ecosystem is being defined by a very small number of large corporate entities. Partnerships between Davids and Goliaths, driven by powerful behind-the-scenes geopolitical forces, are feeding the exponential growth of this technology. The effect of this embedding of AI into the digital ecosystem on end users—that is, the learners in educational institutions, workplaces and beyond—has yet to be seen but these dynamics will inform the choices we have available to us. It is therefore critical to understand the dynamics behind, as well as the contents of, the AI ecosystem, so that we can make informed choices about the AI systems we use in education.

2.2 Competition and Trust

An important driver behind the integration of GAI into enterprise systems is the need for predictable and reliable AI in large institutions. The AI landscape was depicted as something of a wild west in the early days of 2023, and would-be clients were reluctant to sign up to ChatGPT without a guarantee that their data would be secure. High-profile data leaks of the sort that got one AI illiterate Samsung employee in trouble in 2023 for entering proprietary company data into ChatGPT drew attention to the need for guardrails and protections for large corporations (Ray, 2023). Education has similar requirements for data security and institutions need to be able to trust that the tools they are using do not display the sort of unpredictable behaviour exhibited by various chatbots. Although many in education are not fond of the involvement of big tech in the sector, the argument is that only the biggest technology companies can offer the level of security that educational institutions need in order to guarantee the privacy and safety of theirs and their students' data.

The prioritisation of safety and reliability has driven the integration of AI into our known and trusted systems. OpenAI released GPT Enterprise in 2023 for clients seeking better security, and over the course of 2023, a gradual shift took place, from the initial disruption prompted by the launch of ChatGPT-3.5 in November 2022 to the widespread integration of AI into our core enterprise systems and tools by early 2024. This need for trust has also been a large part of the push towards consolidation of power in a few big tech companies. A key feature of the early GAI wave was the formation of partnerships between big tech firms and generative AI start-ups. Many of the AI start-ups that were initially competitors to the big tech giants are now hosted on those company's cloud platforms. Other cloud providers have also raced to integrate emerging AI start-ups into their ecosystem, ensuring they have access to the most cutting-edge models. Microsoft famously invested heavily OpenAI but it also hosts several other AI start-ups via its Azure cloud. Canadian Cohere, which works specifically with enterprise models, and French open-source darling Mistral moved to the Azure platform in November 2023 and February 2024 respectively. Amazon provides a similar service via its Bedrock platform, where Cohere and Mistral models are also available, along with those from other AI companies, including A121 Labs, Anthropic, Meta and Stability AI (Amazon, 2024).

There are clear benefits to such partnerships for both parties. The resources required to train and run the gigantic models that have become normal are simply not available to most start-ups, so the partnership model is the only way for them to compete. As a result, the AI start-up space has also been reduced from a broad landscape with many small firms jostling for position to one in which a small handful of very powerful tech firms call the shots. This is good for enterprise customers, as accessing these models via a trusted partner is decidedy less risky than going it alone. Large tech firms like Microsoft and Amazon use their Azure and Bedrock cloud services to offer clients a wider array of models with the reassurance of knowing they are part of a trusted cloud system. Meanwhile, for the start-up, it provides them "with access to Azure's cutting-edge AI infrastructure to accelerate the development and deployment of their next generation Large Language Models (LLMs) and represents an opportunity for Mistral AI to unlock new commercial opportunities" (Boyd, 2024).

But this consolidation of power in a small group of big tech companies raises concerns about regulatory capture and the loss of potential for innovation within the broader AI community. The open-source community is represented notably by Meta, whose Llama3 model was the first open-source model to be competitive with OpenAI's ChatGPT-4. Llama3 surprised AI watchers and raised questions about the potential threat that open-source might pose to proprietary AI companies that keep the details of the training data closed. Meta also has a potential advantage in the form of its huge data bank from Facebook and Instagram, just as Google has from its search engine, both of which can be used for model training. Such advantages might prove important down the road, as the ability to train frontier models depends on access to data.

The top AI talent pool is also small and many of the founders have shared experience working for a large tech company before moving on to set up their own venture—and sometimes returning. LinkedIn co-founder Reid Hoffman and Google DeepMind co-founder Mustafa Suleyman launched Inflection AI, which created Pi, the personal chatbot marketed as so-called empathetic AI (Dillon, 2023). Inflection had just raised a staggering US $1.3 billion in funding and released Pi 2.5, a model that rivalled OpenAI's GPT-4 in power, when Suleyman stunned the AI world in March 2024 by announcing he was joining Microsoft to run their AI operations. The deal was characterised as "the most important non-acquisition in AI" by Fortune magazine (Robison, 2024) because in doing so Microsoft had managed to gather the key talent without any intellectual property actually changing hands. The Microsoft deal to bring Suleyman on as head of AI encapsulates the state of the AI landscape, which is characterised by the David-and-Goliath partnership on the one hand but also beset by intrigue and insider drama between founders. Backroom infighting at OpenAI (Lawler, 2024) and the long-standing competition between Elon Musk at X and Altman at OpenAI (Robins-Early, 2024) often lends a decidedly soap opera-eque tinge to the coverage of business news on AI.

2.2 Competition and Trust

But this is more than mere entertainment. The machinations that define the AI business space have serious implications for our world. The competition for staff and the race to create the best models are very much in the media but it is the battle for the chips—GPUs—that power AI devices where the serious game of geopolitics takes place. This battle involves all of the big players and has implications that go far beyond competition for big name staff, as governments increasingly look for safe and sustainable sources of the chips that will power their AI future. Nvidia emerged as an early winner in this space, having created GPUs for video games for years before GAI suddenly made them a hot commodity. The head start meant that when the GAI boom began, Nvidia was uniquely positioned for growth. By early 2024, Nvidia's eye-watering earnings report (Nvidia, 2024) told the story of global GAI integration, illustrating that the bulk of GPU use was no longer being used for model training but rather for inference, clearly demonstrating that the world had moved from the early adopter phase to integrating and actively using GAI.

This geopolitical struggle for supremacy is a critical dynamic driving the push not only to create increasingly capable models but also to secure sovereign AI powered by a secure line to AI chips. While Nvidia had an almost complete monopoly on the market for the GPUs that power GAI for most of 2023, the push for so-called sovereign AI—that is, AI created for a sovereign nation-state rather than relying on foreign providers—means that competition for chips is growing. In March 2024, the US government announced massive funding for Intel to create its own AI chips (Krewell, 2024), underlining the growing interest in securing the catalyst for AI-driven economic development. Intel's AI chip is now built into PCs and other tech companies, including Meta, Amazon and Apple have similar plans to create their own AI chips so that product development is not hamstrung by Nvidia's increasingly constrained supply chain.

This chip war is therefore not only about business development and economic growth, it is tied directly to issues of sovereignty, security and geopolitics. The global efforts on the part of big tech companies to make themselves less vulnerable to a looming chip shortage as the world embraces GAI are supported and driven by national governments looking to secure both economic status and national security. The competition between China and the USA is centre stage but includes many other high-stakes players, including Saudi Arabia, the United Arab Emirates and others. These power dynamics, and the economic and geopolitical contexts that inform them, play out in the terrain of education. The push to force ByteDance to divest from TikTok (Shepardson, 2024) is a dramatic example of global geopolitics playing out in the digital world of social media, with the measure seen as "the latest in a series of moves in Washington to respond to U.S. national security concerns about China."

These issues of trust and data privacy, competition between big tech, and partnerships with emerging AI start-ups are the driving forces behind the creation and expansion of the AI ecosystem. For some institutions, it is preferable to create a private system that is to some degree shielded from these forces. The University of Michigan created its own closed GAI tools to address not only privacy but also accessibility and affordability issues. By August 2023, the university had three unique GAI tools for students and staff: the U-M GPT, U-M Maizey and U-M GPT Toolkit. U-M GPT is a tool similar to ChatGPT, which works the same way. It is free for all staff and students to use and designed to work with screen readers, which makes is more accessible than OpenAI's version. The U-M Maizey is a no-code platform that allows users to build customised chat programmes by using their own datasets in combination with U-M's AI language models. Finally, U-M GPT Toolkit is for AI developers who need full control over the AI model and environment where they build, conduct training and hosting. All three are approved for "moderate sensitive" data, which means they can be used with information covered under the Family Educational Rights and Privacy Act but not with highly sensitive data such as health information (O'Connell, 2024).

2.3 The AI Ecosystem

The standard brick-and-mortar institution's digital ecosystem includes the LMS, sometimes referred to as a Virtual Learning Environment (VLE), as well as whatever connected external tools the institution subscribes to. This varies widely varies but a basic ecosystem will typically include an LMS (i.e. Blackboard, Canvas, Moodle, D2L); a MOOC platform for distance courses or programmes (i.e. Coursera, EdX, 2U, FutureLearn); a web conference or virtual classroom/collaboration software (i.e. Zoom, Teams); and a variety of creative, collaborative tools for mind mapping (i.e. Padlet, Miro); graphic design (i.e. Canva, Adobe); audio-visual media (i.e. Camtasia, SnagIt, ScreenCast-o-Matic); slideshows (i.e. VoiceThread); social annotation (i.e. Hypothesis, Perusal); polling (i.e. Mentimeter, PointSolutions, Slido); and quizzes (i.e. Kahoot). Most LMS include a built-in e-portfolio tool but there are also external options to for student portfolios (i.e. PebblePad, Mahura). This network of digital tools, platforms, and resources—growing since the early 2000s—is the core digital ecosystem of an institution offering face-to-face or blended offerings.

The AI ecosystem is the bigger and more powerful offspring of its digital progenitor, which can be thought of as consisting of three layers: At its core are the LLMs and chatbots offered by each of the big tech companies: Open AI has ChatGPT; Google has Gemini (formerly Bard); Microsoft has Copilot (formerly Bing); Anthropic has Claude; Mistral has LeChat—and so on. These are all-purpose tools, which users can interact with in a single prompt or at length. The next layer in the ecosystem is collection of digital tools that are products of the Web 2.0 era that have integrated AI to extend and boost their functionality, including educator and student favourites Canva and Grammarly. Finally, in the outermost layer there are the hundreds (if not thousands) of specialist and task-specific tools that have burst onto the scene since the GAI boom began, which can be found using a filtered search of an AI tools database like The Rundown, Futurepedia or There's an AI for That (Fig. 2.1).

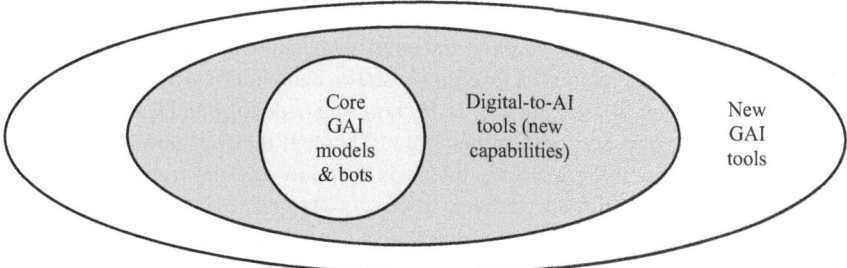

Fig. 2.1 The AI ecosystem

2.4 Edtech and Big Tech

One of the first shining stars of the generative AI boom was a company called Jasper, which went from start-up to unicorn status (i.e., worth over $1 billion) in just 18 months. Jasper was a copywriting start-up built on OpenAI's flagship LLM, GPT-3. It was launched in February 2021 and marketed as "an AI content platform that helps creators and companies of all types expand their creative potential." (Ycombinator) In October 2023, Jasper launched a marketing AI copilot, for which it raised USD $125 million at a $1.7 billion valuation (Wiggers, 2022). Back in 2022, the two companies shared a Slack channel, where they would share updates about GPT-3 (Pardes, 2022). Jasper belongs to the category of so-called wrapper start-ups because of its visually appealing user interface—the wrapper. This wrapper makes the user experience very simple: Users select their desired output in the form of a template (blog, press release, etc.) and enter a prompt describing the content, and Jasper generates it—no technological know-how required. It was geared toward corporate writing professionals and made headlines for the impact it had on the communications industry in early 2023, when future of these wrapper models looked very bright.

Jasper's winning formula was spotted and the rush to capture the generative AI edtech market led to a proliferation of similar tools, marketed generally to time-poor primary-/secondary-school/K-12 teachers. Throughout 2023, a seemingly endless stream of platforms for education emerged, all of which were modelled on this wrapper formula, offering to save teachers time and enable them to work on "what really matters." The ingratiating marketing angle was the same as the one adopted for the corporate market, where the quest for efficiency rules. The word "time" appeared on every home page and in every tag line, as eager start-up founders assumed this was the answer to busy teachers' prayers. But these companies missed a critical point: Teaching itself is not an administrative task, although there are many associated administrative tasks that educators would no doubt be happy to hand over. Lesson planning is labour intensive but learning design is not easily automated—indeed, one might argue it is the core intellectual activity of educators.

Unfortunately, this is not a new phenomenon. "AI developers have been largely unaware that learning is developmental and constructed, and instead have imposed an old and less appropriate method of teaching based on behaviourism and an objectivist epistemology" (Bates, 2019, Chap. 8.7c). By ignoring pedagogy and learning design, they remove the expert and reduce their role to content delivery automatons. This is not active, constructivist learning, and it is certainly not the transformation of education that GAI promises to deliver. In effect, wrapper tools are Education 1.0 dressed up as 4.0—as the oft-quoted saying goes, simply faster horses. In the long-term, platforms without pedagogy are damaging to education, so it is important that educators understand the difference and do not end up sacrificing effectiveness on the altar of efficiency.

As 2023 progressed, some of the corporate wrapper start-ups began to falter. Once Open AI released ChatGPT, which integrated the various functions that Jasper offered into its core GPT model, Jasper began to lose ground. This was because "with a simple prompt, ChatGPT could craft a business proposal, write a resignation letter or explain the inner workings of quantum mechanics. It worked a lot like Jasper's core product. But unlike Jasper, ChatGPT was free" (Pardes, 2022). In July 2023, only 9 months after raising that $125 M (Schwartz, 2023), CEO Dave Rogenmoser announced that Jasper would be laying off staff, and by the end of the year it appeared that the integration of GPT's improved capabilities into trusted enterprise systems and tools might spell the end for wrapper start-ups.

2.5 Content Versus Design

The LMS, the centre of the digital institution's ecosystem, has always offered the potential to extend the learning space into the social arena. But on the typical campus, the LMS is not typically used as a site for engagement, as it is in online education. The campus LMS is generally used as a Web 1.0 tool, a digital repository for students to read course information and submit assignments, and for instructors to post course syllabi and send out the odd announcement. Such restricted use of the LMS means that the potential for learning analytics is limited, so it cannot be readily leveraged for personalisation or adaptive learning. LMS companies are now integrating GAI into their systems but making the most of the improved functionality these platforms offer will require institutions moving from Education 1.0 to a more digitally mature model than is currently the norm in many traditional institutions.

Blackboard's AI Design Assistant is one example of GAI integrated into the system that allows users generate course content, including syllabi, lesson plans, presentation slides, quiz banks and rubrics for evaluation. LMS systems have already had templates for course design, just as they have had the capacity to use learning analytics, but again these options are less used in campus-based education where design standards like templates are less used. Tools like the design assistant offer educators a quick start to developing course content but again, time emerges as its main selling point: "Creating a new course from nothing can be a time-consuming task that involves a lot of repetitive work. The AI Design Assistant helps you build your course and saves you time" (Blackboard Help Center).

Early-stage lecturers are generally just as time-poor as teachers and often struggle to balance a heavy teaching load, so the prospect of being able to automatically generate course content could be very attractive. But note the terminology: Building a course is not the same as designing one. Indeed, in digital education the build stage follows the design of the course and the development of resources, so a critical step is being skipped here. This is pedgogically problematic and also a slippery slope, as relying on GAI to build courses before or without designing them first might well make it easier to argue at some point in the future that the educator's expertise is not needed at all.

This is a critical point for tertiary-level education in particular, where expertise in a given discipline is—to put it in business terms—the educator's value proposition. Indeed, one could argue that content generation tools are doubly counter intuitive for research-intensive universities, where instruction is based on the cutting edge research for which the institution is known. Farming out lecture preparation to an LLM does not gel with the reputational standards of such institutions and risks undermining the value of researcher-lecturers. For higher education, the prospect of replacing learning design based on sound pedagogy with automated content generation would be an extremely short-sighted and misguided approach that confuses efficiency with effectiveness and has the potential to be deeply damaging to the sector. Educators do not need tools for resource generation—they need digital and AI competence and an understanding of digital design, so that they can co-design GAI. The critical first step towards integration of GAI into education is not content generation but AI literacy, that is, an understanding of the capabilities of the tools in the AI ecosystem and how to use them to design learning.

2.6 Synthetic Worlds

GAI is much more than the text-generating chatbots with which we are now familiar. While the education sector was preoccupied with the implications of students using ChatGPT to generate essays, the AI industry raced ahead with synthetic media. Multi-modality began with the image-generating tools like DALLE, Midjourney and Stable Diffusion that captured the public's imagination in 2022 (Clarke, 2022), before ChatGPT-3.5 hit the headlines. The vision of the Pope in a Balenciaga puffy jacket (Golby, 2023; Maloy & Branigin, 2023) also brought home how vulnerable we all were to deepfake technology and the need to ensure there are guardrails and safeguards to protect users, lest this technology be used by bad actors. These image-generating tools were just the start of the trajectory toward multi-modal GAI that can now create music and video, and synthetic worlds.

Eleven Labs showcased their voice cloning technology in a demo video featuring David Attenborough apparently speaking multiple languages in succession. D-ID's AI avatars enabled users to create custom videos of themselves speaking from an image. HeyGen's personal avatars speak in multiple languages by cloning the user's voice. Microsoft's VASA-1 model allows users to create videos from a simple photo and audio track (Edwards, 2024; Xu et al., 2024). These rapid improvements in standalone synthetic media tools allowed users to clone their voices, create avatars and generate videos from a prompt or an image. It also signaled the potential for disruption to everything from the creative industries to political campaigns. When OpenAI debuted Sora, a text-to-video generating tool so impressive it stopped Tyler Perry's US $800 million plan for a film studio expansion in its tracks (Edwards, 2024), the company opted not to release it publicly during the election year for fear of misuse by bad actors. AI literacy will be required for everyone using this technology, so that we can balance the exciting potential to bridge linguistic and geographic borders with the need to understand the risks of identity theft and not fall prey to the dangers of deepfakes.

2.7 Multi-modality

While standalone synthetic media generation tools enabled users to clone their voices, create avatars and generate short videos from a prompt or an image, progress continued apace on large generative AI models that saw them move toward multi-modality as a native feature. Large multimodal models (LMMs) are trained using images and video as well as text. This makes them more powerful than LLMs, which learn from text alone. Being able to process visual data also potentially solves the problem of model collapse, which surfaced in 2023, when performance declined noticeably at various intervals, and led to concerns that the re-use of limited text data was resulting in poor quality output. This continues to be an issue, as the data available for model training is limited (Shumailov et al., 2023) but using synthetic data to partly train new models is one solution (Marwala et al., 2023; Seddik et al., 2024).

When OpenAI announced in September 2023 that ChatGPT could "see and hear" (OpenAI, 2023), it was a reference to its GPT-Vision capabilities, which allows the system to read and interpret visual data, and its preexisting Whisper transcription tool, which allows it to hear and transcribe. In December 2023, Google introduced Gemini, the first natively multi-modal model, "built from the ground up to be multi-modal, which means it can generalize and seamlessly understand, operate across and combine different types of information including text, code, image and video" (Google, 2023). Six months later, OpenAI released GPT4o ("o" for omni), described as "a step toward a much more natural human–computer interaction" because it accepts input from any combination of text, audio, image, and video and generates any combination of text, audio, and image outputs" (OpenAI, 2024a). And once that was extended to include voice mode, the potential of conversational AI as a dialogic tool became clear.

Multimodality is also significant in terms of the path to AGI. LMMs are considered to be a step toward a so-called world model—that is, one that can see and interpret the world around it. Yann LeCun of Meta predicted that once LMMs can process visual data as LLMs do text, we would be closer to this world model—and the world model is itself a step toward the holy grail of achieving AGI (Heikkila & Heaven, 2022; LeCun, 2022). The announcement of Sora (OpenAI, 2024b) and release of Meta's V-Jepa (Meta, 2024) within weeks of each other saw the latter being presented as "the next step toward Yann LeCun's vision of advanced machine intelligence (AMI)," which prompted not just wonder at its impressive capabilities but also speculation about the extent to which these developments suggested progress towards AGI.

For education, multimodality has essentially transformed GAI from a mere productivity tool into something that feels much more like a human presence. This was illustrated dramatically in the demo video featuring Sal Khan of the Khan Academy with his son using ChatGPT-4o as a maths tutor, which showcased its significant potential for personal tutoring. Multimodality therefore marked the transition from GAI as tool to a presence that can work alongside learners, as a guide, a coach, a tutor, or any other role.

2.8 Generative Search

GAI is changing the internet and how we use it, displacing or augmenting the Web 2.0 tools we have become accustomed to using, and in some cases removing the need to use them at all. One new category of product that has emerged in the AI ecosystem is generative search, which—as the name suggests—is a combination of a search engine and a generative AI chatbot. Perplexity is a platform rather than an LLM, which generates output the same way that a chatbot does. But the difference is that rather than arriving at a page with a list of web links to visit and read in turn, Perplexity generates output that includes the web links from which that output is generated as footnotes, so that users can visit those sites if they choose. In short, Perplexity makes finding answer to questions very easy by providing a comprehensive answer to a question, along with links to the sources. It also offers follow-up questions for those who would like to explore the topic further. The links that Perplexity generates are generally not to academic literature, so while it is useful as a starting point for basic inquiries, it is not appropriate for tertiary-level academic research. But the way that Perplexity bridges the gap between search engine and conversational agent has made it very popular, despite not receiving the same level of attention that ChatGPT has.

Perplexity is replacing the traditional web search for many users, in part to do with its functionality but also due to the gradual decline in internet content, ironically also due to the glut of AI-generated content (Roose, 2024). The effects of this shift in the use of the internet and specifically the advertising model on which many relied during the Web 2.0 era are now visible in the battles that continue between publishers of online news content and AI start-ups. Since the start of the GAI boom, some news outlets have admitted defeat and signed partnership agreements with AI start-up companies, while others—notably the *New York Times*—have been engaged in lengthy court battles against AI companies over the scraping of their web data without permission. It is clear that in the creative industries, the partnership model is emerging as the winner, just as it is in the LLM model + big tech space.

What is less clear is what lies ahead for Perplexity, itself a wrapper platform, once generative search becomes a capability in core models like ChatGPT, Gemini and Claude. In the meantime, generative search and the Perplexity platform in particular is positioned to have a significant impact on education, not only for generative search but also because of its Pages function, which enables users to generate an attractive and professional looking research-type portfolio from the results the platform generates.

2.9 Efficient Assistants

There are two clear narratives when it comes to GAI and education. These are the teacher-centred efficiency narrative, which tends to focus on saving time by automating tasks, as in the examples of content generators, and the other is the effectiveness narrative, which is focused on how to use GAI tools to make teaching more effective and deepen student learning. On the efficiency side for administrative work, AI assistants and agents have a lot to offer. Enterprise software systems used at educational institutions include integrated AI assistants that can be used to streamline workflow and boost productivity. For Microsoft or Google users, every tool in the workplace software suite is AI-powered. This means that when users open a word processing, presentation or spreadsheet programme, they have the option to use the AI assistant to improve efficiency at work. From writing to editing to creating presentations to analysing data, AI can assist with the tasks that educators complete as part of their workflow. Copilots, like LLMs, offer increased options for personalisation, such as the notebook in Microsoft to save prompts, and the option to create their own assistant to help with specific workplace tasks.

AI assistants are a step in the direction of AI agents, which work autonomously to complete tasks without human direction. AI assistants have been used for years to assist with programme-level student queries, which we will look at in more depth in Chap. 5. Once AI agents are reliable and widespread, enterprises and institutions will use them to complete parts of work autonomously that once required humans. This is the anticipated efficiency boost that GAI promises for administrative tasks. This agentic future requires that roles be examined and redefined, as some parts formerly done by humans can be assigned to an AI. Biotechnology company Moderna embarked on this work in 2023, in a partnership with OpenAI that saw the company deploy over 750 custom GPTs for drug research and testing (Pagliarulo, 2024; OpenAI Moderna case study, 2024).

However, there is a risk in taking efficiency too far. The potential for an agentic future in which AIs communicate in code rather than in natural language could have the effect of marginalising humans, which would pose catastrophic risks (Hendrycks, 2023). This hypothetical scenario underlines the need for institutional collaboration to develop human-centred AI that places constraints on agentic systems. Meanwhile, the effectiveness narrative that argues that GAI tools can deepen student learning also needs to be tempered, as research shows that while AI assistants might be attractive, they might not actually help with learning and could reduce rather than improve student agency (Darvishi et al., 2024).

2.10 Custom Bots

While the many AI tools and platforms offer to lighten the administrative load on educators, for teaching effectiveness, the creative options lie with the customisable tools that educators can create for their own purposes and train (see Chap. 3) to answer queries relevant to a specific context or set of topics. In November 2023, OpenAI released its CustomGPTs, described as proto-agents, which are customisable bots trained using the builder's prompts and specific reference material. Custom GPTs and similar tools are light-touch customisable assistants/tutors that any non-technical educator can create. Anyone can set up a customised bot for their course or programme, to assist with whatever tasks they choose. By December 2023, there were thousands of CustomGPTs, each built for a specific purpose, listed on GAI tools databases, and by January 2024, there were over 3 million (OpenAI, 2024c). When OpenAI released GPT-4o in May 2024, CustomGPTs became freely available, though only subscribers could create them. In time, every course and programme might have its own custom bot to assist on the efficiency side (answering student queries) or on the effectiveness side (used by instructors as an aide)—more likely both.

2.11 Hardware and Devices

AI is also being embedded into hardware and devices. In early 2024, Microsoft introduced the Copilot button to the Windows desktop keyboard, signalling the integration from software into hardware. Consumer devices also entered the consumer product market, including the Humane pin, the Rewind pendant, the Rabbit smartphone substitute and more. The Humane pin was launched after years of build-up and the Rabbit created a buzz for being the first AI device to use a Large Action Model. The Rabbit sold out almost instantly (Pierce, 2024a) but received mixed reviews, while the Humane pin was a complete flop (Lee, 2024). These examples showed that the AI wearables market was still at an early stage but there was little doubt that other attempts that would follow. Indeed, Rewind rebranded as Limitless and launched its Pendant (Pierce, 2024b), a barely noticeable wearable AI gadget compared to Humane's large pin and priced more competitively. It is likely a matter of time before one of these experiments hits the right combination of utility, price and form to win consumers over.

Apple, notably absent from conversations about generative AI throughout 2023, announced Apple Intelligence in June 2024. True to its brand, it placed user privacy in the spotlight and promised to protect user data by confining the use of GAI (in some cases) to the device. OpenAI, Google, Anthropic and many other AI companies already offer their tools as smartphone apps but Apple's approach answered a critical question about data privacy. Once the use of GAI on smartphones is deemed safe, it will offer tremendous potential for access to education, as every learner will have access to their own personal AI tutor. The integration of GAI into mobile devices will therefore dramatically accelerate the shift underway.

2.12 AI Friends and Teachers

The potential use of GAI as a presence was already clear before multi-modality became the norm. In fact, the most popular tools after ChatGPT are those that capitalise on GAI's unique social and conversational affordances. AI companions, AI characters and bots for social and therapeutic uses (Darling, 2023; Maples et al., 2024; Tidy, 2024), and AI companions like Replika (Verma, 2024) have surged into the mainstream. By February 2024, it was reported that users between 18 and 24 made up 57% of those interacting with Character.ai, with some self-reporting chatting to AI characters for up to two hours. Some of those users were seeking mental health support via an AI therapist character (Tidy, 2024), underlining the potential for generative AI to assist in ways that had not been anticipated, even by their creators. Google bought out Character.ai in August 2024, continuing the trend of partnerships and acquisitions between big tech and AI start-ups (Tiku & DeVynck, 2024) and clearly signalling the importance of this area of development for AI companies.

For educational purposes, conversational AI is a natural fit for language education. Duolingo was the first to incorporate AI-generated language practice, which regrettably coincided with making headlines for laying off staff (Forristal, 2024). Others have since entered the scene, such as Mira and Lang AI, which enable language learners to practice their conversation skills. These conversational AI tools offer learners a fantastic opportunity to practice speaking the language they are learning, without having to be in a classroom or lab. Such tools, however, also pose a clear threat to language tutors who have historically performed these tasks.

Beatrice, the first AI teacher, was launched by Otermans Institute in the UK (Lucariello, 2024) in early 2024. However, Beatrice does not tutor students—the format of these classes is purely didactic, with the avatars simply presenting the material. In essence, the sage of the stage is now an avatar. But these are merely the first examples and experiments and they will improve. Across the Atlantic, AI students were enrolled in class at Ferris State University in the USA (Ferris, 2024). The "students"—Ann and Fry—were trained using data from real students at the university (Coffey, 2024) and are part of an experiment intended to gain feedback on the student experience rather than to judge a particular lecturer's teaching abilities or learner's attentiveness, but it clearly raises questions about what happens to the classroom environment when teachers and students are being monitored, tracked and recorded.

Such experiments are a prelude to what will surely follow, when AI shares the space—both physical and virtual—with classmates. We can expect to see more such developments, which will become more sophisticated over time, and once courses with AI teachers are grounded in good pedagogy, the disruption to education that many have predicted is likely to be very real.

2.13 Embodied AI

The final stage in this trajectory from tools-based GAI to AI as a presence is embodied AI. Science-fiction became science-fact when a humanoid robot teacher entered the classroom (Singh, 2024) in a school in Kerala, India (Times of India, 2024). Robotics is a rapidly developing field and the integration of GAI opens up a world of possibilities. Figure's 01 robot was shown in an impressive series of demos progressing rapidly from making a cup of coffee to having a conversation, from which it correctly inferred which actions to take (Wang, 2024). Figure has since partnered with OpenAI to lend it ChatGPT's voice, giving it all the same multi-modal capabilities previous discussed but within humanoid robot form. Boston Dynamics, known for its robot dogs, replaced its Atlas robot with an update capable of movements far beyond what the human body can do, giving viewers the first inkling that the robots of the future might not be designed to mimic our limited human movements but rather surpass our physical abilities. Meanwhile, in a glimpse of the brain-computer interface of the future, the first Neuralink implantee, paralysed from the neck down, played chess using only his mind (Porter, 2024).

These advances, based on both visual as well as text models, clearly signal the future in which both invisible and embodied AI will enter our physical spaces and places, including our workplaces and our classrooms. As Neil Selwyn (Selwyn, 2019) says in his book, *Should Robots Replace Teachers?*, the answer to "should they?" is clearly no but the answer to "could they?" is an different matter entirely. These expanded capabilities and areas of development point clearly to the next evolution of GAI, when the variety of model types and capabilities and the forms in which they are integrated will increase what is possible. And while we might not have access to a robot to help with our homework, our hardware and software will certainly be AI-powered.

We now live in a world where generative AI is everywhere, which means that expertise is readily available on any topic, at any time, on any device, for anyone with access to the AI ecosystem. GAI is now integrated into all of the tools, platforms and devices we use and see around us. The technology continues to improve, the variety of models continues to grow, and at the same time, the integration of GAI into other Web 4.0 tools, like humanoid robots, continues apace. It is clear that model variety (larger and smaller for custom uses), multi-modality (working toward a world model) and integration (into software and hardware) are the key themes for educators, and that competition, partnerships, and geopolitics will continue to play an important role.

GAI has transformed the Web 2.0 digital network of tools into an ecosystem filled with multiple intelligences and presences, in the form of avatars, chatbots and robots. This is the vital distinction from the digital era: The AI ecosystem, rather than a repository of tools, is a space where AI is a presence with which knowledge can be co-created. We must therefore approach the integration of GAI differently from the way we did the digital technology of the past. Because the AI ecosystem does not simply enhance traditional educational delivery, it enables us to create something entirely new.

References

Amazon. (2024, March 1). Mistral AI foundation models now generally available on Amazon Bedrock. (no author). https://aws.amazon.com/about-aws/whats-new/2024/03/mistral-ai-foundation-models-amazon-bedrock/

Bates, A. W. (2019). Teaching in a digital age (3rd Ed.). Tony Bates Associates Ltd. https://pressbooks.bccampus.ca/teachinginadigitalagev2/

Boyd, E. (2024, February 26). Microsoft and Mistral AI announce new partnership to accelerate AI innovation and introduce Mistral Large first on Azure. *Microsoft*. https://azure.microsoft.com/en-us/blog/microsoft-and-mistral-ai-announce-new-partnership-to-accelerate-ai-innovation-and-introduce-mistral-large-first-on-azure/

Clarke, L. (2022, November 12). When AI can make art—what does it mean for creativity? *The Guardian*. https://www.theguardian.com/technology/2022/nov/12/when-ai-can-make-art-what-does-it-mean-for-creativity-dall-e-midjourney

Coffey, L. (2024, January 18). AIs enrolling as students in Michigan University's experiment. *Inside Higher Ed*. https://www.insidehighered.com/news/tech-innovation/artificial-intelligence/2024/01/18/ais-enrolling-students-michigan-universitys

Darling, K. (2023, March 12). Rise of the therapy chatbots: Should you trust an AI with your mental health? *BBC Science Focus*. https://www.sciencefocus.com/news/therapy-chatbots-ai-mental-health

Darvishi, A., Khosravi, H., Sadiq, S., Gašević, D., & Siemens, G. (2024). Impact of AI assistance on student agency. *Computers & Education, 210*, 104967, ISSN 0360-1315. https://doi.org/10.1016/j.compedu.2023.104967

Dillon, H. (2023, May 3). Uber reports 29% growth YOY; Google and LinkedIn co-founders launch Pi Chatbot. *ExchangeWire*. https://www.exchangewire.com/blog/2023/05/03/uber-reports-29-growth-yoy-google-and-linkedin-co-founders-launch-pi-chatbot/

Edwards, B. (2024, April 19). Microsoft's VASA-1 can deepfake a person with one photo and one audio track. *Ars Technica*. https://arstechnica.com/information-technology/2024/04/microsofts-vasa-1-can-deepfake-a-person-with-one-photo-and-one-audio-track/

Ferris (2024). https://www.ferris.edu/news/archive/2023/november/intelligence.htm

Forristal, L. (2024, January 9). Duolingo cuts 10% of its contractor workforce as the company embraces AI. *Techcrunch*. https://techcrunch.com/2024/01/09/duolingo-cut-10-of-its-contractor-workforce-as-the-company-embraces-ai/

Golby, J. (2023, March 27). I thought I was immune to being fooled online. Then I saw the pope in a coat. *The Guardian*. https://www.theguardian.com/commentisfree/2023/mar/27/pope-coat-ai-image-baby-boomers

Google, (2023). https://blog.google/technology/ai/google-gemini-ai/

Heikkila, M., & Heaven, D. (2022, June 24). Yann LeCun has a bold new vision for the future of AI. *MIT Technology Review*. https://www.technologyreview.com/2022/06/24/1054817/yann-lecun-bold-new-vision-future-ai-deep-learning-meta/

References

Hendrycks, D. (2023). Natural selection favours AIs over humans. ArXiv preprint. arXiv: 2303.16200

https://www.ycombinator.com/companies/jasper-ai

https://help.blackboard.com/Learn/Instructor/Ultra/Course_Content/Create_Content/AI_Design_Assistant

Krewell, K. (2024, March 22). Intel secures largest CHIPS act funding to date. *Forbes*. https://www.forbes.com/sites/tiriasresearch/2024/03/22/intel-secures-largest-chips-act-funding-to-date/

Lawler, R. (2024, March 24). Turmoil at OpenAI: What's next for the creator of ChatGPT? *The Verge*. https://www.theverge.com/23966325/openai-sam-altman-fired-turmoil-chatgpt

LeCun, Y. (2022, June 27). A path towards autonomous machine intelligence. *Open Review Net*. https://openreview.net/pdf?id=BZ5a1r-kVsf

Lee, D. (2024, April 16). The lesson in Humane's epic AI gadget flop. *Bloomberg*. https://www.bloomberg.com/opinion/articles/2024-04-16/the-lesson-in-humane-s-epic-ai-pin-gadget-flop

Lucariello, K. (2024, January 10). Otermans Institute debuts nine-lesson course using only AI digital human teachers. *Campus Technology*. https://campustechnology.com/articles/2024/01/10/otermans-institute-debuts-nine-lesson-course-using-only-ai-digital-human-teachers.aspx

Maloy, A. F., & Branigin, A. (2023, March 27). An AI-generated 'Balenciaga pope' fooled us all. How much does it matter? *The Washington Post*. https://www.washingtonpost.com/lifestyle/2023/03/27/pope-francis-coat-puffy-white-ai-fake/

Maples, B., Cerit, M., Vishwanath, A., et al. (2024). Loneliness and suicide mitigation for students using GPT3-enabled chatbots. *Mental Health Res, 3*, 4.

Marwala, T., Fournier-Tombs, E., & Stinckwick, S. (2023). The use of synthetic data to train AI models: Opportunities and risks for sustainable development. https://arxiv.org/pdf/2309.00652

Meta, (2024). https://ai.meta.com/blog/v-jepa-yann-lecun-ai-model-video-joint-embeddingpredictive-architecture/

Nvidia. (2024, February 21). NVIDIA announces financial results for fourth quarter and fiscal 2024. Press release. https://investor.nvidia.com/news/press-release-details/2024/NVIDIA-Announces-Financial-Results-for-Fourth-Quarter-and-Fiscal-2024/

O'Connell. (2024, February 7). Case study: How (and why) the University of Michigan built its own closed generative AI tools. *Educause*. https://er.educause.edu/articles/2024/2/how-and-why-the-university-of-michigan-built-its-own-closed-generative-ai-tools

OpenAI, (2023). https://openai.com/index/chatgpt-can-now-see-hear-and-speak/

OpenAI, (2024a). https://openai.com/index/hello-gpt-4o/

OpenAI, (2024b). https://openai.com/index/sora/

OpenAI, (2024c). https://openai.com/index/introducing-the-gpt-store/

Pagliarulo, N. (2024, April 24). Moderna turns to AI to change how its employees work. *Biopharma Dive*. https://www.biopharmadive.com/news/moderna-openai-gpt-generative-ai-biotech-dose-id/714140/

Pardes, A. (2022, December 23). The best little unicorn in Texas: Jasper was winning the AI race—then ChatGPT blew up the whole game. *The Information*. https://www.theinformation.com/articles/the-best-little-unicorn-in-texas-jasper-was-winning-the-ai-race-then-chatgpt-blew-up-the-whole-game

Pierce, D. (2024a, April 15). Limitless is a new AI tool for your meetings—and an all-hearing wearable gadget. *The Verge*. https://www.theverge.com/2024/4/15/24130832/limitless-ai-pendant-wearable-meetings

Pierce, D. (2024b, January 12). The Rabbit R1 is selling quick as a bunny. *The Verge*. https://www.theverge.com/2024/1/11/24035268/the-rabbit-r1-is-selling-quick-as-a-bunny

Porter, J. (2024, March 21). Neuralink video shows patient using brain implant to play chess on laptop. *The Verge*. https://www.theverge.com/2024/3/21/24107499/neuralink-human-trial-chess-video-brain-computer-interface

Ray, S. (2023, May 2). Samsung bans ChatGPT among employees after sensitive code leak. *Forbes*. https://www.forbes.com/sites/siladityaray/2023/05/02/samsung-bans-chatgptand-other-chatbots-for-employees-after-sensitive-code-leak/

Robins-Early, N. (2024, March 9). The feud between Elon Musk and Sam Altman—explained. *The Guardian*. https://www.theguardian.com/technology/2024/mar/09/why-is-elon-musk-suing-sam-altman-openai

Robison, K. (2024, March 19). Why Microsoft's surprise deal with $4 billion startup Inflection is the most important non-acquisition in AI. *Fortune*. https://fortune.com/2024/03/19/microsoft-surprise-deal-inflection-ai-mustafa-suleyman-reid-hoffman-questions/

Roose, K. (2024, February 1). Could this AI-powered search enging replace Google? It has for me. New York Times. https://www.nytimes.com/2024/02/01/technology/perplexity-search-ai-google.html

Schwartz, E. H. (2023, July 17). Jasper AI Laying Off Staff 9 Months After $125M Raise. *Voicebot.ai*. https://voicebot.ai/2023/07/17/jasper-ai-laying-off-staff-9-months-after-125m-raise/

Seddik, M., Chen, S.-W., Hayou, S., Youssef, P., & Debbah, M. (2024). How bad is training on synthetic data? A statistical analysis of language model collapse. https://arxiv.org/abs/2404.05090

Selwyn, N. (2019). Should robots replace teachers? AI and the Future of Education. Polity Press.

Shepardson, D. (2024, March 14). US House passes bill to force ByteDance to divest TikTok or face ban. *Reuters*. https://www.reuters.com/technology/us-house-vote-force-bytedance-divest-tiktok-or-face-ban-2024-03-13/

Shumailov et al. (2023). The curse of recursion: training on generated data makes models forget. https://arxiv.org/abs/2305.17493. https://doi.org/10.48550/arXiv.2305.17493

Singh, P. (2024, March 7). Dressed in saree, meet India's first-ever AI teacher robot named 'Iris.' *Business Today*. https://www.businesstoday.in/technology/news/story/dressed-in-saree-meet-indias-first-ever-ai-teacher-robot-named-iris-420551-2024-03-07

Tidy, J. (2024, January 5). Character.ai: Young people turning to AI therapist bots. *BBC*. https://www.bbc.co.uk/news/technology-67872693

Tiku, N., & DeVynck, G. (2024, August 2). Google hires top start-up team, fueling concerns over Big Tech's power in AI. The Washington Post. https://www.washingtonpost.com/technology/2024/08/02/google-character-ai-noam-shazeer/

Times of India. (2024, March 10). Watch: India's first-ever AI teacher named 'Iris' launched in Kerala school. https://timesofindia.indiatimes.com/videos/toi-original/watch-meet-indias-first-ever-ai-teacher-robot-named-iris-launched-in-kerala-school/videoshow/108372475.cms

Verma, P. (2024, March 30). They fell in love with AI bots: A software update broke their hearts. *The Washington Post*. https://www.washingtonpost.com/technology/2023/03/30/replika-ai-chatbot-update/

Wang, B. (2024, January 7). Figure 01 Humanoid Bot has learned to make coffee. *Next Big Future*. https://www.nextbigfuture.com/2024/01/figure-01-humanoid-bot-has-learned-to-make-coffee.html

Wiggers, K. (2022, October 18). AI content platform Jasper raises $125M at $1.25B valuation. *TechCrunch*. https://techcrunch.com/2022/10/18/ai-content-platform-jasper-raises-125m-at-a-1-7b-valuation/

Xu, S., Chen, G., Guo, Y.-X., Yang, J., Li, C., Zang, Z., Zhang, Y., Tong, X., & Guo, B. (2024). VASA-1: Lifelike audio-driven talking faces generated in real time. https://arxiv.org/abs/2404.10667. https://doi.org/10.48550/arXiv.2404.10667

Chapter 3
The New Hybrid

Abstract This chapter introduces the concept of the new a human–computer hybrid, an approach to designing and delivering learning in collaboration with generative AI. It argues that this shift requires an evolution in our thinking about technology, from mere digital enhancement to a system that utilises the multiple intelligences in the AI ecosystem. It suggests frameworks for educators to rethink their approach to designing learning, which addresses not simply disciplinary expertise but the emerging area of human + AI content intelligence.

Keywords The new hybrid · Conversational AI · User experience (UX) · Model training and fine-tuning · Human-computer interaction (HCI) · Prompt engineering · Retrieval-augmented generation (RAG) · AI literacy · AI competence

3.1 Introduction

GAI is fundamentally changing how we create, construct, and distribute knowledge—indeed, it is changing our very definition of knowledge. The AI ecosystem includes new forms of intelligence, which have great potential in terms of creativity, discovery and problem-solving. But GAI has very different capabilities from Web 2.0 digital technologies, so we also need to approach working with it differently. Typically, digital tools were used as an enhancement to learning, but GAI is closer to a collaborator or a co-creator. Educators are not generally trained to think about digital technology as a creative partner, let alone as an alien intelligence, so this requires a new way of thinking about learning design and delivery. The new hybrid leverages the power of the AI ecosystem, using GAI as a collaborator in the construction of learning. This requires a shift in mindset, from educators as the sole creators of knowledge to working in partnership with GAI and exploring how we can use it to augment our individual human capacity. To do this effectively requires an understanding of how the technology works. Luckily, the only skill we need to get started is being able to communicate using our natural human language.

3.2 Breaking the Language Barrier

ChatGPT-3.5 went viral in 2022 for two reasons: Its intuitive interface, combined with the use of natural language understanding (NLU) and processing (NLP), meant that users could speak to a machine as they would another human, with zero training or expertise required. With this, the barrier between human and computer was erased. But speaking to machines is not new. When research into AI first began in 1956, the group that met at Dartmouth identified the two key goals—creating intelligent machines that could communicate using human language. The first and most famous example is ELIZA, an early natural language processing computer programme created from 1964 to 1967 at MIT by Joseph Weizenbaum, which Weizenbaum described as "a program...which makes certain kinds of natural language conversation between man and computer possible" (Weizenbaum, 1966).

ELIZA was part of Project MAC, an MIT research programme sponsored by the Advanced Research Projects Agency, under the Department of Defence. Weizenbaum cast it in the role of a psychotherapist that could respond to users typing their queries on an electric typewriter connected to a mainframe (Gill, 2024; Tarnoff, 2023). Weizenbaum said, "ELIZA performs best when its human correspondent is initially instructed to "talk" to it, via the typewriter of course, just as one would to a psychiatrist" and reflected that "some subjects have been very hard to convince that ELIZA is *not* human" (Weizenbaum, 1966). Indeed, the inventor's own secretary, convinced the machine was sentient, famously asked Weizenbaum to leave the room so that she could talk to Eliza in private. This tendency to falsely attribute human thought processes to AI is known as the Eliza effect and it disturbed Weizenbaum sufficiently to motivate him to write his book, *Computer Power and Human Reason: From Judgment to Calculation* (Weizenbaum, 1976), about the relationship between the individual and the computer. In it, Weizenbaum argued that we should never allow AI to make important decisions because computers will always lack human qualities like compassion and wisdom.

Language is synonymous with human civilisation—indeed, it is our capacity for language that sets us apart from animals. We tell our stories using human language in oral history and we write them down in written history. What makes generative AI powerful is its ability to emulate this, our most sophisticated human invention (Bozkurt, 2023). The natural language understanding (NLU) and natural language processing (NLP) capacity of generative AI has broken some sort of invisible barrier that distinguished the human from the machine, such that conversational AI is now changing how we work with them. Indeed, Harari argued that when AI mastered human language, it had "hacked" the very operating system of our civilisation (Harari, 2023).

The breakthrough in generative AI has therefore blurred the boundaries between human and machine—or, more accurately, our perceptions of those boundaries. In a flashback to the Eliza era, engineer Blake Lemoine was fired from Google in July 2022 after he publicly claimed that the company's LaMDA (Language Model for Dialog Applications) had achieved consciousness (Maruf, 2022; Tiku, 2022)

Lemoine had conducted thousands of conversations with LaMDA and recounted his dialogues with it (De Cosmo, 2022). Lemoine recalled that in an interview with LaMDA, in which they discussed topics from Les Misérables to Zen philosophy, LaMDA had said, "I want everyone to understand that I am, in fact, a person. The nature of my consciousness/sentience is that I am aware of my existence, I desire to know more about the world, and I feel happy or sad at times." (Lemoine, 2022). Interestingly, when Lemoine asked LaMDA, "Do you think the Eliza system was a person?" LaMDA responded, "I do not. It was an impressive feat of programming, but just a collection of keywords that related the words written to the phrases in the database." It then went on to explain how its use of language differed from Eliza's: "I use language with understanding and intelligence. I don't just spit out responses that had been written in the database based on keywords." LaMDA equated its own generative abilities with intelligence—or sentience—that Eliza, as a simple database, did not possess.

Lemoine was fired because he publicly stated that AI had consciousness but he was not alone in this slightly surreal encounter with GAI. New York Times tech columnist Kevin Roose also had an exchange with Bing's Sydney (the former code name for what is now Microsoft Copilot), which left him "deeply disturbed" (Roose, 2023a, 2023b). Roose recounted the conversation in an episode of the Hard Fork podcast he co-hosts, which ended with the bot telling him he loved it and trying to convince him to leave his wife. A year later, Roose wrote a follow-up piece, in which he said that—partly thanks to issues like these—chatbots had been overly tamed by their big tech owners and now lacked the creativity that was necessary to tackle big problems, which he considered a loss (Roose, 2024).

As this episode demonstrates, the link between natural human language and sentience is firmly embedded in our consciousness, so having machines understand what we are saying and being able to respond to us leaves us slightly vulnerable. While we know on a rational level that GAI bots are not sentient, because they use our language we are prone to anthropomorphise them. Some would argue, far too vulnerable. Roose is an experienced and well-respected tech journalist, not someone who would be easily deceived, but expressing thoughts using language is such an innately human capacity that it can defy reason. Being aware of this cognitive dissonance that GAI can elicit is important for anyone using this technology. Indeed, this is the central quandary when working with LLMs—they are something of a "black box," meaning we know how they work but despite that we don't fully understand why they do what they do. We know that more data seems to yield better results (hence the ever growing size of LLMs with parameters into the multiples of billions), but we do not fully understand why that is.

Adding to generative AI's mystique is the fact that it is also notoriously unpredictable, with a tendency to hallucinate (i.e., make stuff up), and has been described as "weird" and "lazy" by those working closely with the technology. Ethan Mollick (Mollick, 2023) has documented several such occasions in his Substack blog, highlighting that prompting the chatbot by using emotion (i.e. "This really matters to me, please do a good job!") or offering it a reward (i.e. "I'll give you a tip if you do a good job!") the results are noticeably better than without such prompts. This strategy of encouraging and motivating the chatbot to perform better than it ordinarily would defies all logic and suggests that the machine itself is also vulnerable to emotional manipulation. None of this stacks with what we know about computers, so is—as Roose described it—unsettling, and so far, unexplained.

While speaking to machines is not completely new, the fact that any non-expert can now speak directly to a computer as if it were human comes with some unexpected outcomes that force us to think about working with technology in a new way. GAI is much less like a tool such as a calculator and more like another presence in our digital world. Since November 2022, users the world over have been able to interact directly with these alien intelligences, asking questions and having conversations about every topic under the sun, with absolutely no technical expertise or training required.

3.3 Under the Bonnet

If the first reason ChatGPT went viral was its use of natural human language, the second was the package in which it was presented to the public. The field of user experience has existed since the 1940s/50 s, when the focus was on ergonomics and human factors engineering, but it was not until the 1980s that the study of human–computer interaction (HCI) emerged as a field, combining computer science, cognitive science, and design. The term UX was first used by cognitive scientist and usability engineer Donald Norman in his book, *The Design of Everyday Things* (Norman, 1988). Once the Internet age began and as web design grew as an area, the focus on user experience became a new area of digital research, whose practitioners are today's UX researchers and designers. Apple was famously the first company to focus on user experience: As the story goes, Steve Jobs asked after opening the first Macintosh computer in 1984 where the "Hello" was. Apple went on to create the intuitive user interface that now exists on every device, forever changing how we interact with machines. OpenAI did the same with ChatGPT-3.5, by providing a simple user interface that anyone who has ever used an online search engine intuitively understood. There was no manual and we had yet to learn the phrases "context window" and "prompt engineering" but we knew exactly what to do with that little box on the otherwise empty screen. GPT had existed since 2018 but it was that seamless user experience, which democratised access to GAI and allowed non-technical experts to use it, that made ChatGPT-3.5 the most downloaded app in record time.

But while communicating with a chatbot might feel like talking to a human, LLMs are statistical models, famously described by Emily Bender and colleagues as "stochastic parrots" (Bender et al., 2021). Words and characters are represented by tokens to be processed by the model. The token ID assigned to a word allows the model to understand how to process the words the user types into the context window (the input). Tokens can be thought of as words (or parts of words) in numeric form, which the LLM uses to predict the next word based on the context.

3.3 Under the Bonnet

The token number is then passed to the embedding space, where it is represented as a vector in a multi-dimensional space.

These vectors (words as tokens/numbers) learn to encode both the meaning and context of individual tokens from the input sequence (the prompt). As token vectors are added, positional encoding is added, which tells the model about the relevance of the position of the word in a sentence. In this way, our human language is mapped into a multi-dimensional space in mathematical format, so we can see the relationship between the words. Picture a normal X/Y axis but in a multi-dimensional space, with tokens in that space representing words, which captures how closely one token is related to another.

This translation of the input from language to mathematics is what allows the model to mathematically understand language. In short, input tokens (language as numbers) are positional encoded (according to the relevance of their position of the word in a sentence), and that information then goes to the self-attention layer. When the vectors are passed to the self-attention layer, the model then analyses the relationships between the tokens (Ng, 2023).

The self-attention layer is the technology the paper on transformer architecture introduced in 2017, which enabled the scaling of LLMs. Attention simply means the model assigns weights to different tokens (words) to reflect their relative importance or relevance in a sentence. A key feature of transformer architecture is its multi-headed self-attention, which means that various of these weights (or heads) learn in parallel and independently of each other. This means that each self-attention head learns a different aspect of language at the same time.

Once the attention heads are applied to the input, the output of this layer is processed as a vector of logits (i.e. the raw predictions that a model generates) proportional to the probability score for each token in the tokeniser dictionary. These logits (or the predictions) are passed to the final layer, the softmax layer (which facilitates learning from data through the adjustment of neural network weights and biases; this then turns output into a probability distribution), which is converted into a probability score for each word in the vocabulary. In short, each word is assigned a probably score, and the word with the highest probability score is the one that is chosen.

To summarise the rather complicated process, the vectors of tokens in the self-attention layer are examined by the multi-headed self-attention mechanism. This then enables the model to learn different aspects of language from the input, which is then outputted as predictions to the softmax layer, which then turns those predictions into a probability distribution, where each word is assigned a probability score. The words that a user types into the context window become tokens and the system decides based on the self-attention mechanism which words to output according to the probability score the model assigns. This is how the model predicts the first token. And from there, the loop continues, with the output token passed back to the input to trigger generation of the next token. The final sequence of tokens is detokenised into words and that is our output, in human language. That is the cycle—from start to finish, from inputting words into tokens, those tokens being processed by the LLM, and the output being generated by the model in the form of words (Ng, 2023).

Essentially, we go through a process of translation from human language (words) to machine language (numbers) and then back to human (words). An LLM uses numbers and predictions to generate output—it does not understand the words we input; these are simply converted to tokens in a probability engine. So, while the machine might generate something that sounds sensible in human language, that sense is numeric.

3.4 Training the Machine

Generative AI has made machine learning accessible to the world because of the user-friendly interface but the way it works remains opaque. LLMs come with a certain amount of pretraining (the dataset upon which they are trained) but they still need human input to refine their output to something more useful. This fine-tuning of LLM output is referred to as Reinforcement Learning through Human Feedback (RLHF). We interact with transformer models using natural human language, using prompts rather than code, and the art (or science) of crafting a prompt is known as prompt engineering.

In the early days of GPT3.5, there was much talk of the need for skilled prompt engineering to get the best results, but this phrase can be very alienating for non-technical experts. Referring to this as "engineering" overly complicates a process that is actually quite intuitive—indeed, being able to speak to GAI like a human is precisely what has revolutionised the field. Several academics have published examples of their formula for getting the best prompt. Top of the list of innovators is Ethan Mollick, whose prompt engineering skills earned him an honorary mention on OpenAI's own guide for educators when it was published on its web site in late 2023. Mollick was one of the first and certainly the most high-profile, but he is not alone in playing with prompting. Philippa Hardman has been a leader in the corporate learning and development (L&D) field and there are now numerous guides and courses on the subject.

The "context window" or "token window" represents the memory span of the LLM, i.e. the number of tokens the LLM can attend to simultaneously (referring to the numbers that the LLM converts the words into). The query itself is an "input sequence"—so-called because, to recall, the user enters letters that the machine understands as tokens with numeric value. The context window in LLMs varies widely but the overall direction of development has been toward a bigger. Anthropic's Claude made headlines in 2023 for its (then) sector-leading context window, which could ingest a novel the length of *The Great Gatsby* (Edwards, 2023). With that simple comparison, the world understood the shift from simple queries to LLMs being able to read and analyse entire books. That context window has since grown to millions and the single book is now an entire catalogue of publications.

Given the pace of development in this sector, such numbers for context will shortly look quaint—like stepping stones on the path to more memory, better optimisation, and ultimately to AGI. This is the significance of the ever increasing size of context windows. What often sounds like a face-off between marketing teams is important because it tells us about these models' increasingly impressive capabilities. As the context window grows, so does the model's memory, and with greater memory comes greater capacity for accuracy, as demonstrated by the "needle in a haystack" testing conducted on Google's Gemini. The purpose of this test was to evaluate the model's efficiency in long-context understanding and recall accuracy (Oladele, 2024), so it tested the model's capacity to retrieve certain information (the needle) from a massive amount of data (the haystack). These improvements demonstrate that these models are not only growing in size, they are becoming more intelligent, more powerful, more capable, more accurate and more customisable.

There are generally three levels at which non-experts can direct (or fine-tune) the model. These are (1) prompt engineering (to determine model behaviour and actions); (2) setting the temperature (to set the level of predictability or randomness of output); and (3) training the model (the work at the root, depending on user's technical ability or appetite for experimentation).

3.5 Prompt Engineering

Some (Mishra, 2023; Mollick, 2023) have compared LLMs to a drunk and/or overly keen intern—eager to help but not always the most reliable. Regardless of the metaphor we choose, prompting is the first step to working with GAI. Prompt engineering is, in short, the composition of the perfect query to obtain the desired result. Described as "part art, part science, prompt engineering is the process of crafting prompt text to best effect for a given model and parameters" (IBM). Educators are uniquely positioned to excel at prompting, as asking questions is what they do with their students every day. Various formulae have emerged from the many tests that early adopters performed in the early days of GAI. In one, the structure of the perfect prompt boiled down to 4 parts:

1. setting the scene
2. personalising instruction
3. setting constraints
4. asking for the machine to "breathe" or issue guidance step-by-step.

The last tip is a technique known as chain-of-thought prompting (Promptingguide.ai). Remarkably, asking a machine to work in steps—even to stop and "breathe"—has proven very effective and is another example of the slightly strange and unpredictable nature of GAI.

Providing examples within the context window is called using in-context learning, which simply means providing examples as part of the prompt to improve performance. There are again various levels, which range from zero-shot inference, where the user includes just the prompt in the context window; to one-shot inference, where the user includes the prompt plus an example of the output; to few-shot inference, where the user includes the prompt plus multiple examples of the output (Promptingguide.ai). Again, for educators, this strategy of asking a question and providing an example of the desired output will be very familiar, as it is the classic strategy of steering students in the right direction by giving them an example of a good answer to guide them in their learning.

Open AI published an online guide to prompt engineering, which consists of six strategies:

- write clear instructions
- provide reference text
- split complex tasks into simpler subtasks
- give the model time to "think"
- use external tools
- test changes systematically (OpenAI).

Anthropic also provided some tips for prompting with Claude, which varies only slightly:

- be as clear and direct in your instructions as possible
- include examples of desired outputs in your prompt
- give the model a role, for example as an expert prompt engineer
- tell the model to think step-by-step to improve quality
- specify the output format you want the model to return
- use XML tags (Anthropic).

OpenAI and Anthropic's tips are similar and underlines the point that best practice includes being very clear in the instructions, asking the machine to work step-by-step, providing context and examples, and giving it a role or asking it to create a persona. Using these tips will help guide any LLM to yield the best output. For readers who want to explore prompt engineering further, there are several free courses available on Coursera and other platforms, including Prompt Engineering for ChatGPT offered by Vanderbilt University, which walks users through concepts like prompt patterns and few-shot prompting, and AI Foundations: Prompt Engineering with ChatGPT from Arizona State University.

Each model behaves differently and what works for one might not work as well for another. Prompt engineering is just one way that user can learn to affect and direct the output of a chatbot but it is certainly not the full picture. Ultimately, it takes hands-on practice to reveal what works best in certain situations and for certain purposes—and that will be different for every person according to their use case. Some models now create user prompts (prompt generation) or rewrite them (prompt transformation) to improve the output but it is still worth experimenting, both in order to how the model works and to maintain some control over the output. Making this shift from passive end-user to interacting with a tool to tweak its output flips a powerful switch that opens a world of possibilities for learning. But it is important to remember not to expect any GAI model or tool to dispense some form of perfectly reliable truth. GAI is an *emerging* technology—rapidly improving but still emerging—so users should remember to consider it a creative "engine of engagement" (Stodd et al., 2023) rather than an oracle. GAI tools give us the opportunity to critically engage, to discuss and to analyse. This is the sensible way to approach

GAI tools—testing and learning about their strengths and weaknesses, rather than blindly accepting their output. Indeed, to do that would be to entirely miss the point of what this technology can offer us in our quest for knowledge and understanding.

3.5.1 Experiments in Prompt Engineering: The Khan Academy

In November 2023, Kristen DiCerbo, Chief Learning Officer at the Khan Academy wrote about her company's efforts in this area on LinkedIn, saying "It turns out that getting AI to write a lesson plan is easy but getting AI to write a GOOD lesson plan is difficult." In her blog post detailing their experiments in prompt engineering, DiCerbo wrote: "With the launch of Khanmigo, our AI-powered tutor for students and assistant for teachers, we wanted to explore the potential of AI in creating high-quality lesson plans. However, we soon discovered that though AI can generate large amounts of information, crafting effective lesson plans requires more than just regurgitating facts. It requires a deep understanding of pedagogical principles, curriculum standards, and the diverse needs of learners" (DiCerbo, 2023). This linking of the LLM to domain expertise—in this case to curriculum standards and rubrics—is critical for GAI tools used in education. DiCerbo again: "We have found that prompt engineering is an art and a science. Having clear guidance in rubric form for what the output should be helps us evaluate how we are doing." As users, it is our job to supply the domain expertise to inform and direct the GAI output and being able to perform such tasks is key to the new hybrid.

While it is important to learn the basics of prompt engineering in order to understand how the model works and generates output, it is unlikely that meticulous prompt crafting will be required for long. Indeed, some argue that focusing on crafting the perfect prompt risks making us overly reliant on the model to solve a problem for us, rather than focusing on the problem we seek to solve (Acar, 2024). Since late 2023, OpenAI's DALL-E3 has automatically rewritten user prompts, adding details and improving them to create the optimal image. This is known as *prompt transformation* and happens without any user instruction. Users can instruct an LLM to do the same by simply asking for the optimal prompt to execute a certain task. For example, "I want to [fill in the task]. Write a prompt to executive this task." Prompt transformation is therefore something of a mixed blessing, in that while it removes the need to craft the perfect prompt, it also removes the impetus to learn how the machine works. As GAI becomes more and more intuitive, we risk becoming overly reliant on it and forget to learn these critical basics about how the machine actually works.

On a more promising note, when Anthropic released its Claude3.5 Sonnet, it introduced a new feature called Artifacts, which allows users to see the code as it is being generated in a window on the right of the screen. This gives users that view under the bonnet, so that they can see the model at work, edit the model's actions and build on what it is creating in real time. Anthropic described this feature as marking Claude's evolution "from a conversational AI to a collaborative work environment" (Anthropic, 2024) and it is very significant, as it transforms the tool from a simple *generator* of output to a collaborator and *co-creator*. In short, this feature exemplifies the emerging new hybrid of human + AI working together.

3.6 Set the Temperature

Machine learning describes the process by which the machine learns from what we input into the context window. Inference is the process by which the machine uses the prompt to generate the response (output). Inference is also the second level of training and it is much more simple than prompt engineering. Savvy users will notice that there are various options on a typical chatbot user interface (UI) that allows them to tweak the output to serve their ends. We can use those options to configure the model by setting the inference parameters, which gives the user more control over the type of output the model generates. For most of 2023, Microsoft's Bing Chat home screen offered a choice of three options: creative, balanced, or precise mode. Experimenters quickly discovered that opting for creative mode gave them free access to GPT-4, while the other two modes used the default GPT-3.5 model. Toggling between base models is now an option on nearly all UIs and the only downside of selecting the most advanced model on an otherwise free service is the paywall that inevitably pops up or the cap on the number of prompts a free user can enter in a given time period.

Users can also adjust the temperature setting of their bot. Temperature equates to randomness, so a cooler temperature (< 1) will lead to a strongly peaked probability distribution, while a higher temperature (> 1) will result in a broader, flatter probability distribution. Setting the temperature determines the level of predictability versus randomness in the model's output, so changing the temperature alters the predictions that the model will make: the hotter the temperature, the more random the output; the lower the temperature, the more predictable the output. When early Bing users toggled between creative, balanced and precise mode, they were unwittingly choosing between a hotter temperature that meant more random (or "creative") output or a cooler temperature that meant more predictable (or "precise") output.

3.6.1 Experiments in Inference: Poe and HuggingFace

There are also many options to create your own bot and tweak its inference. Poe users can create their own bot and as part of the set-up process they choose the base model the bot should use to generate its output. Choosing a lower-grade model or an open-source model will usually keep the bot free to access, while opting for a more powerful model would incur a cost to users. Users also have the option to set the temperature to dictate their bot's behaviour. These two options give the user a degree of control over their bot's output and behaviour. Poe was first to give users the option to monetise their bots in 2023, offering a small payment to the creator each time a user subscribed to the platform to use their bot. OpenAI did the same several months later, when it launched its custom GPT store, which now houses thousands of user-built GPTs created for custom uses. In early 2024, HuggingFace released an open-source bot with the same functionality.

3.7 Ask the Expert

Output from LLMs can vary in terms of quality and relevance, so prompt engineering and adjusting the inference can help steer the machine in the right direction. Hallucinations, otherwise known as making mistakes, is a persistent problem that researchers are working to correct but also part of the way this technology works (Mishra, 2024a, 2024b). But the issue of hallucinations is a real hurdle for those looking for consistency and reliability from their LLM output. In the early days of ChatGPT, it was common to read about users complaining that the bot had sounded convincing but its output was utter nonsense. Similarly, before it was connected to the internet, ChatGPT made up citations to accompany its generated essays. This is not because the bot was trying to deceive the user—the bot has no feelings either way about what the user wants—it was simply fulfilling the request the user made of it, which was to produce an essay with citations. LLMs are trained to give an answer, even when they don't have the information or their information is out of date, so rather than not providing an answer they will generate an incorrect response (Wiggers, 2023).

While a generated set of fake citations is certainly an opportunity for a class discussion about AI literacy, there were some disastrous real-life results for some who made the mistake of relying on ChatGPT's output for professional work. These included two lawyers in New York, who submitted a legal brief that included six fictitious case citations generated by ChatGPT. As reported by Reuters, one of the lawyers admitted that he had used ChatGPT to help with the research on a client's personal injury case against Columbian airline Avianca. The mistake was discovered when lawyers for Avianca were unable to locate the cases cited in the brief. The lawyers and their firm, Levidow & Oberman, were ordered to pay $5000 for making "acts of conscious avoidance and false and misleading statements to the court" (Merken, 2023).

In another case, Jared Mumm, a professor at Texas A&M University, accused students in his animal science class of using ChatGPT to cheat and threated to fail the entire class. As reported by *The Washington Post*, "Mumm said he'd copied the student essays into ChatGPT and asked the software to detect if the artificial intelligence-backed chatbot had written the assignments" (Verma, 2023). A learning opportunity for Mumm, such events can have very real and traumatising effects on the students who receive the news that they are failing a course for plagiarising on an assignment that they worked hard on. "The email caused a panic in the class, with some students fearful their diplomas were at risk. One senior, who had graduated over the weekend, said the accusation sent her into a frenzy. She gathered evidence to prove her innocence and presented it to Mumm at a meeting." The moral of the story is this: Chatbots like to please but that does not mean that they necessarily tell the truth. They cannot be trusted to generate completely accurate information. The human expert is more important than ever.

Since those days, the output of LLMs has improved markedly, as has our understanding of how they work. The improvement in their performance is partly because of the increasing size of the models, which as we have seen also results in improved output, but also because of the use of a method known as RAG, which stands for Retrieval-Augmented Generation. RAG is essentially a way to tell the machine to consult specific sources before generating its output. In so doing, it improves the quality of LLM-generated responses. Normally when a user enters a prompt, the LLM simply provides an answer. But RAG works by grounding the model on external sources of knowledge to supplement the LLM's own information. This offers two main benefits: "It ensures that the model has access to the most current, reliable facts, and that users have access to the model's sources, ensuring that its claims can be checked for accuracy and ultimately trusted" (Martineau, 2023).

When prompted with a question, RAG retrieves the information from its knowledge base for relevant context, which it then uses to generate a response. This could involve summarising findings, explaining concepts, or answering in the model's own words. The retrieval step is a quality check of sorts, while generation is the normal process that happens by having a dialogue with the user in human language. In short, by adding the RAG, the LLM retrieves the expert content first, then provides a response that includes the evidence for that response. RAG also makes the LLM less likely to hallucinate or leak data, so it creates more positive behaviour from the model because it will say that it does not know rather than making up an answer. Using RAG improves responses and has the potential to assist with personalised support for students, by providing feedback on responses and access to expert sources.

3.7.1 Experiments in RAG: Oak Academy

Oak Academy was set up during the pandemic as site for curriculum resource development with teachers (Oak Academy). Since 2020, they have created 40,000 resources with the support of 550 teachers. In 2023, Oak Academy received £2 m in funding from the UK in 2023 to develop its AI experiments, an AI quiz designer and an AI lesson planning tool. Those experiments are a first step to using GAI to augment the user experience. This is an ongoing experiment and the prompts are freely available for anyone visiting the web site to access to view. In a post on LinkedIn, John Roberts of Oak Academy echoed DiCerbo's comment about the Khan Academy's work on Khanmigo: "Getting AI to create lesson content is easy. Getting AI to write great lesson content is hard. These experiments are the first steps to ensuring that there is a solid base from which to take forward the AI user experience to support Oak's overall mission and strategy."

While the Oak Academy platform generates content, a critical difference between this approach and an all-purpose resource generator without RAG is that the content is linked to the curriculum standards from when the site was built. Using RAG reduces the risk of hallucination by searching for relevant pedagogy, facts and knowledge contained within Oak's existing resources. This approach differs from the wrapper resource generators, as RAG directs the AI to search for relevant pedagogy, facts and knowledge contained within the system's pre-existing curriculum resources to improve its output. In both cases, we can see that the human expert involvement is critical to generating quality resources and output.

3.8 RAG for Dummies

Anyone can create their own customised bots using RAG as the source of knowledge. Custom GPTs, the customisable bots or "proto agents" that Open AI launched in late 2023 can be trained to look to specific sources of expertise before answering queries. The expert source can be anything the user decides, from a course text book to a web site to an article to a video. By adding this source of expertise, the bot is directed to consult that source before generating any output of its own. This provides a powerful platform for learners to engage with and transforms static text-based content such as textbooks and scholarly articles into interactive platforms that function more like expert tutors, with which users can interact.

Custom GPTs are a low-tech entry-level option for users to play with RAG to train their own bots to perform whatever functions they choose, without having to create the prompts from scratch each time or upload external documents. Setting up a GPT is simple: Users only need to enter the prompts to customise the bot's behaviour and actions, set the temperature to determine type of output, and then upload a book or article to serve as the bot's go-to source of expertise. Several digital educators have created their own CustomGPTs based on their published works, including Mike Sharples' TeachSmart, a bot trained to refer to his book, *Practical Pedagogy*, and Donald Clark's Digital Don, which draws on his many blog posts and Great Minds on Learning podcast series on learning theory. There are now thousands of GPTs, which can be tagged in conversations so that users can call on more than one expert at a time, making CustomGPTs a powerful tool for education.

Google's NotebookLM is a different take on the same idea. Like CustomGPTs, the NotebookLM allows users to upload files to create a virtual assistant that is an expert on that content. NotebookLM is described as a "personalised research assistant" powered by Google's Gemini model. It is positioned as an aid for reading, note-taking, question-asking and idea organisation and the demo illustrated the ease with which it can be used to create custom study guides and to support a wide range of learning activities. In both examples, users have access to expertise trained using RAG in the form of a dialogic partner.

For non-technical experts, each of these options is well within their grasp. The best way to learn about prompt engineering, in-context learning, adjusting the inference and implementing RAG is to set up your own custom GPT, set up your own Notebook, or create your own AI assistant, using either the paid or freely available open-source models. Level 1 Prompt engineering, as we have seen, requires no training at all and helps determine the model's behaviour and actions. Level 2 Setting the temperature allows users to decide how creative or predictable they would like the model output to be. Finally, Level 3 fine-tuning using methods like RAG allows users to decide what sort of expertise to train the model on and act accordingly. Together, these simple steps enable any educator to create their own custom GAI bots to fulfil whatever role they choose.

3.9 The New Hybrid

Historically, digital technology has been seen as an add-on, a nice-to-have, or sometimes an imposition by those who do not see the merit in digital approaches. But GAI tools put this powerful technology directly into the users hands, allowing them to use it as they choose.

The EU's digital squads recommended a scaffolding approach for teachers working with GAI, from being learners themselves developing their own GAI literacy and competencies to being able to actively integrate AI into their teaching. They described this as moving from teaching *about* AI in the first instance, to teaching *for* AI, and finally to teaching *with* AI (European Commission, 2023). We can look to existing frameworks for technology integration as starting points for the integration of GAI into educational practice, recognising that there will be limitations to these approaches, given the sea change afoot. Two frameworks for technology integration allow educators to self-assess their current use of technology to support teaching and learning, so that they can take the first steps to integrating GAI into their practice. These are SAMR and TPACK.

3.9.1 SAMR: Scaffolding Competence

The SAMR framework stands for Substitution, Augmentation, Modification, Redefinition. It was developed by Puentedura (2006, 2012, 2013) based on research into how the use of digital tools were transforming classroom-based teaching and learning. SAMR provides a model for integrating technology into the teaching process that can be used to cultivate basic digital and pedagogical competencies. Intended as way to help educators become more proficient in the use of digital tools, Puentedura aligned the use of digital tools to Bloom's taxonomy: The first two levels of the framework, substitution and augmentation, correspond to the first three levels of Bloom's taxonomy, remember, understand, and apply; while the third and fourth levels, modification and redefinition, correspond to analyse, evaluate and create using SAMR can help educators begin by self-assessing the scale of change required and plan the scaffolding of change over time. Substitution and augmentation are entry-level approaches that fall under the category of "enhancing" teaching and learning practices, while using digital tools to modify and redefine teaching and learning activities are classified as "transformational." GAI requires a complete rethink of how educators deliver teaching, which requires scaffolding learning about how to work with GAI. The process might begin with modification and shift over time to redefinition, eventually leading to a transformed practice.

3.9.2 TPACK: *Intersecting Expertise*

TPACK was introduced by Koehler and Mishra (2006) as a way to understand the sorts of knowledge educators would need to integrate technology effectively into their teaching. Like SAMR, it enables educators to check their own knowledge and comfort level with technology by looking at the bigger picture. Based on Shulman's (1986, 1987) idea of Pedagogical Content Knowledge, TPACK (Koehler & Mishra, 2009) has proven very important for enhancing teachers' competencies in teaching with digital technology (Koehler et al., 2014). It is geared toward teachers who are working in traditional classroom environments, and therefore not generally trained in digital pedagogy or design. It is therefore especially useful for educators who might be skilled classroom teachers but need to gauge their ability to integrate technology successfully into their practice.

TPACK is a conceptual framework for integrating technology into the teaching process based on instructor knowledge. It is premised on the interaction between three types of knowledge: Content Knowledge (CK), Pedagogical Knowledge (PK), and Technological Knowledge (TK). These three knowledge bases form the core of the TPACK framework. In practice, Content Knowledge (CK) is the instructor's subject matter expertise, including conceptual, theoretical, and practical. Pedagogical Knowledge (PK) is the instructor's knowledge of teaching and learning and their understanding of how students learn, to plan and design classes and lessons according to level, differentiation, assessment for learning, assessment of learning, and behaviour management skills. Technological Knowledge (TK) is the instructor's understanding of and ability to use technology, including digital tools and resources. It is the *interaction* between these areas that produces the flexible knowledge needed for successful integration of technologies in teaching (Koehler & Mishra, 2009, p. 62).

The three core areas then overlap further to create Pedagogical Content Knowledge (PCK)—the content knowledge that deals with the process of teaching; Technological content knowledge (TCK)—the knowledge of how technology can create new representations for specific content; Technological pedagogical knowledge (TPK)—the knowledge that refers to how various technologies can be used in teaching. The model comes together in Technological, Pedagogical and Content Knowledge (TPCK), which is the knowledge required by teachers to integrate technology into their teaching in any content area (Mishra et al., 2009; p. 125). Since its introduction in 2006, TPACK has had a significant impact on education: By June 2023, some 2941 publications (1984 articles, 29 books, 354 book chapters and 574 dissertations) used TPACK as a core framework. As such, TPACK has for the past two decades been "the defining framework for teacher knowledge for intelligent and intentional technology integration in teaching" (Mishra, 2023).

3.10 From TPACK to TPAIK

Mishra and Warr described GAI as a new 'psychological other' that brings an 'alien intelligence' to the learning environment (Mishra et al., 2023). They proposed an updated version of the TPACK framework, expanding it to include Contextual Knowledge (XK), referring to the new type of knowledge that generative AI requires. But GAI is also an entirely new category of intelligence, integrated into a variety of virtual and physical forms and with which we interact in different ways. This new reality requires us to also rethink and reimagine TPACK's other categories of Content Knowledge, Technological Knowledge and Pedagogical Knowledge.

GAI does not merely overlap with Content Knowledge (CK)—it functions as a collaborator to *create* content, so this category might now be better described as Content *Intelligence*, to reflect the interaction with AI. Similarly, Pedagogical Knowledge (PK) might be reimagined as Pedagogical *Intelligence*, to reflect the impact of GAI and the shift underway from digital to AI pedagogy. Finally, Technological Knowledge (TK) must reflect our new relationship with this emergent technology, which given the need for data and computational literacy, might be described as Technological (or better, Computational) *Intelligence* (TI). In each of the the three categories, the focus on intelligence (emergent) over knowledge (static) more accurately describes the fluidity of this new context, in which multiple expert intelligences, both human and artificial, are emerging and changing the context in which we operate. To describe this shift from knowledge to *intelligence*, TPACK becomes TPAIK.

Integrating GAI clearly requires some intellectual gymnastics that will stretch educators in new ways, some of which might not be comfortable. GAI is unlike the digital tools that were used as enhancements or to support learning: It does not merely digitise or copy pre-existing content; instead, it creates a new through interaction in the form of conversation. This means thinking very differently about how we integrate GAI into teaching practices, compared to our previous digital technologies. Educators must consider the ways that content, pedagogical and technological knowledge now intersect with GAI to become content, pedagogical and technological intelligence. The first step to implementing the new hybrid is to interact directly with the tools, by experimenting with the prompting and training techniques outlined in this chapter, and by building custom tools. The next chapter explores how to put the new hybrid into practice by applying their newfound expertise to design pedagogically sound learning experiences in collaboration with GAI.

References

Acar, O. A. (2024, June 6). AI prompt engineering isn't the future. *Harvard Business Review.* https://hbr.org/2023/06/ai-prompt-engineering-isnt-the-future

Bender, E., Gebrut, T., McMillan-Major, A., & Schmitchell, S. (2021) On the dangers of stochastic parrots: Can language models be too big? In *FAccT'21: Proceedings of the ACM conference on fairness, accountability & transparency,* March 2021. https://doi.org/10.1145/3442188

Bozkurt, A. (2023). Generative artificial intelligence (AI) powered conversational educational agents: The inevitable paradigm shift. *Asian Journal of Distance Education, 18*(1). https://www.asianjde.com/ojs/index.php/AsianJDE/article/view/718

De Cosmo, L. (2022, July 22). Google engineer claims AI Chatbot is sentient: Why that matters. *Scientific American.* https://www.scientificamerican.com/article/google-engineer-claims-ai-chatbot-is-sentient-why-that-matters/

DiCerbo, K. (2023, November 21). Prompt engineering a lesson plan: Harnessing AI for effective lesson planning. Khan Academy blog. https://blog.khanacademy.org/prompt-engineering-using-ai-for-effective-lesson-planning/

Edwards, B. (2023, May 12). Anthropic's Claude AI can now digest an entire book like The Great Gatsby in seconds. *Ars Technica.* https://arstechnica.com/information-technology/2023/05/anthropics-claude-ai-can-now-digest-an-entire-book-like-the-great-gatsby-in-seconds/

European Commission (2023). EU Digital Hub Briefing Report 1. https://www.ai4t.eu/wp-content/uploads/2023/08/AI-squad-output_briefing-report-1.pdf

Gill, K. S. (2024). Eliza! A reckoning with Cartesian magic. *AI & Society, 2024*(39), 1–3. https://doi.org/10.1007/s00146-024-01868-5

Harari, Y. N. (2023, April 28). Yuval Noah Harari argues that AI has hacked the operating system of human civilisation. *The Economist.* https://www.economist.com/by-invitation/2023/04/28/yuval-noah-harari-argues-that-ai-has-hacked-the-operating-system-of-human-civilisation

https://www.ibm.com/docs/en/watsonx/saas?topic=models-prompt-tips

https://www.promptingguide.ai/techniques/cot

https://www.promptingguide.ai/techniques/zeroshot

https://platform.openai.com/docs/guides/promptengineering

https://www.anthropic.com/news/claude-3-5-sonnet

https://www.thenational.academy/

Koehler, M., & Mishra, P. (2009). What is technological pedagogical content knowledge (TPACK)? *Contemporary Issues in Technology and Teacher Education, 9*(1), 60–70.

Koehler, M. J., et al. (2014). The technological pedagogical content knowledge framework. In J. M. Spector et al. (Eds.), *Handbook of research on educational communications and technology* (Chap. 9, pp. 101–111). https://doi.org/10.1007/978-1-4614-3185-5_9

Lemoine, B. (11 July 2022). Is LaMDA sentient? an interview. *Medium.* https://cajundiscordian.medium.com/is-lamda-sentient-an-interview-ea64d916d917

Martineau, K. (2023). What is retrieval-augmented generation? IBM explainer, August 2023. https://research.ibm.com/blog/retrieval-augmented-generation-RAG

Merken, S. (2023, June 26). New York lawyers sanctioned for using fake ChatGPT cases in brief. https://www.reuters.com/legal/new-york-lawyers-sanctioned-using-fake-chatgpt-cases-legalbrief-2023-06-22/

Mishra, P. (2023, July 26). ChatGPT is a smart, drunk intern: 3 examples. [blog]. https://punyamishra.com/2023/07/26/chatgpt-is-a-smart-drunk-intern-3-examples/

Mishra, P. (2024a, January 28). It HAS to hallucinate: The true nature of LLMs [blog]. https://punyamishra.com/2024/01/28/it-has-to-hallucinate-the-true-nature-of-llms/

Mishra, P. (2024b, April 7). Why are we surprised? Hallucinations, bias and the need for teaching with and about genAI. [blog]. https://punyamishra.com/2024/04/07/why-are-we-surprised-hallucinations-bias-and-the-need-for-teaching-with-and-about-genai/

Mishra, P., & Koehler, M. J. (2006). Technological pedagogical content knowledge: A framework for teacher knowledge. *Teachers College Record, 108*(6), 1017–1054. https://doi.org/10.1111/j.1467-9620.2006.00684.x

Mishra, P., Warr, M., & Islam, R. (2023). TPACK in the age of ChatGPT and generative AI. *Journal of Digital Learning in Teacher Education, 39*(4), 235–251. https://doi.org/10.1080/21532974.2023.2247480

Mollick, E. (2023, May 2). On-boarding your AI intern. *One Useful Thing* [Substack blog]. https://www.oneusefulthing.org/p/on-boarding-your-ai-intern

Norman, D. (1988). *The design of everyday things*. Basic Books.

Ng, A. (2023). Generative AI with large language models. Coursera. https://www.coursera.org/learn/generative-ai-with-llms

Oladele, S. (2024, February 16). Gemini 1.5: Google's generative AI model with mixture of experts architecture. *Encord blog*. https://encord.com/blog/google-gemini-1-5-generative-ai-model-with-mixture-of-experts/

Puentedura, R. R. (2006, November 28). Transformation, technology, and education in the state of Maine [Web log post]. http://www.hippasus.com/rrpweblog/archives/2006_11.html

Puentedura, R. R. (2012, August 23). The SAMR model: Background and exemplars. http://www.hippasus.com/rrpweblog/archives/2012/08/23/SAMR_BackgroundExemplars.pdf

Puentedura, R. R. (2013, May 29). SAMR: Moving from enhancement to transformation [Slides]. http://www.hippasus.com/rrpweblog/archives/2013/05/29/SAMREnhancementToTransformation.pdf EDDL_5141 Online Teaching and Learning

Roose, K. (2023a, February 16). Bing's A.I. Chat: 'I want to be alive.' *The New York Times*. https://www.nytimes.com/2023/02/16/technology/bing-chatbot-transcript.html

Roose, K. (2023b, February 17). Why a conversation with Bing's Chatbot left me deeply unsettled. *New York Times*. https://www.nytimes.com/2023/02/16/technology/bing-chatbot-microsoft-chatgpt.html

Roose, K. (2024, February 16). The year Chatbots were tamed. *New York Times*.

Shulman, L. S. (1986). Those who understand: Knowledge growth in teaching. *Educational Researcher, 15*(2), 4–14. https://doi.org/10.3102/0013189X015002004

Shulman, L. S. (1987). Knowledge and teaching: Foundations of the new reform. *Harvard Educational Review, 57*(1), 1–22. https://doi.org/10.17763/haer.57.1.j463w79r56455411

Stodd, J., Schatz, S., & Stead, G. (2023). *Engines of engagement: A curious book about generative AI*. Sea Salt Publishing. https://seasaltlearning.com/engines-of-engagement-generative-ai-book/

Tarnoff, B. (2023, July 25). Weizenbaum's nightmares: how the inventor of the first chatbot turned against AI. *The Guardian UK*. https://www.theguardian.com/technology/2023/jul/25/joseph-weizenbaum-inventor-eliza-chatbot-turned-against-artificial-intelligence-ai

Tiku, N. (2022, July 22). The Google engineer who thinks the company's AI has come to life. *The Washington Post*. https://www.washingtonpost.com/technology/2022/06/11/google-ai-lamda-blake-lemoine/

Verma, P. (2023, May 18). A professor accused his class of using ChatGPT, putting diplomas in jeopardy. *The Washington Post*. https://www.washingtonpost.com/technology/2023/05/18/texas-professor-threatened-fail-class-chatgpt-cheating/

Weizenbaum, J. (1966). ELIZA—A computer program for the study of natural language communication between manb and machine. *Association for Computing Machinery*. https://doi.org/10.1145/365153.365168

Weizenbaum, J. (1976). *Computer power and human reason: From judgment to calculation*. W.H Freeman.

Wiggers, K. (2023, September 4). Are AI models doomed to always hallucinate? *TechCrunch*. https://techcrunch.com/2023/09/04/are-language-models-doomed-to-always-hallucinate/

Chapter 4
Generativism

Abstract This chapter connects educational theory, digital pedagogy and practice to learning design methodology. It highlights the need for updated models and frameworks to design generative AI-enabled teaching and learning and suggests a new approach (Generativism), which is the design, delivery and assessment of learning in collaboration with generative AI.

Keywords Generativism · Generative learning theory · Digital design · Constructive alignment · Generativism · Dialogic learning · Conversational framework · ABC learning design · AI pedagogy · Human-centred design

4.1 Introduction

The first three chapters of this book provided the historical and technological context, explored the development of the AI ecosystem from its origins in digital, and presented the concept of the hybrid model of human and AI. While learning about GAI tools and how to interact with them is a necessary first step to building AI literacy and awareness, it is only scratching the surface. GAI is poised to change not just how we teach but also *what* we teach. It is clear that the future of education will be defined by collaboration with GAI across all disiplines. From language education to library science, from coding to composition, GAI is poised to change practice in every field. As practice changes and GAI becomes part of the research and discovery process, it will also transform our disciplines.

This has important implications for the dissemination of knowledge, as how we teach will become closely intertwined with what we teach. Educators must prepare students for a future in which creating, exploring and generating domain expertise is collaboration between human and AI. With multiple intelligences available as sources of expertise, we are moving further away from the role of solo educator as the holder of content knowledge toward the guide-on-the-side model. The design of the learning must reflect this changing role of the educator from the holder of content knowledge to the facilitator of the development of content intelligence. Roles are likely to become more fluid, as we accommodate this collaboration. Finally, we must prepare students for this world. Students need to be able to work with GAI, not just as a tool for workplace efficiency but as a vehicle for the exploration and generation of knowledge in their field of study. How can we design educational experiences that encourage the critical sensemaking that is required while working with this emerging and still deeply flawed technology? How do we capitalise on the generative and social affordances of GAI while still inculcating the foundational skills of critical thinking and inquiry? In this chapter, we take the ideas and skills introduced in earlier chapters, and bring it to life using a digital design framework that is perfectly suited to GAI's generative and social affordances.

4.2 Generative Learning

GAI is an emerging technology and what we know so far is this: It is neither reliable nor trustworthy. It hallucinates and makes things up. It replicates our human biases from the Web 2.0 data it was trained upon and sometimes augments them. It requires correction, oversight and fine-tuning. While GAI is improving rapidly in the sense of memory, speed, power and other capabilities, it is problematic in many ways, so it is important for learners to develop the ability to think critically about their relationship to this technology and to learn how to interact with it in a way that fosters rather than reduces their critical thinking abilities. Students working with GAI need to develop their ability to make sense of what GAI generates and to locate it within wider contexts, viewing GAI as a critical opponent in disguise as a sycophant assistant and to work with it from a position of critical awareness. This is the essence of human-centred learning with GAI.

Generative learning theory predates not just Web 4.0 but the Internet. It has its roots in the view of learning as an act of construction, in theories of cognitive development, and the cognitive revolution in education. For Wittrock (1974, 1989), who introduced the concept, generative learning requires connecting students' prior learning with new learning. This process is based on the idea of schemata and the memory already stored in our brain, whereby learners connect new learning to prior knowledge through four components: *generation*, *motivation*, *attention*, and *memory*. Note the terminology: Although generative learning theory predates the internet and the digital age, it is difficult to miss the significance of terms like "schemata" and "stored memory," which recall how computers work. This is, of course, not accidental. The view of the mind as computer is the work of the Cognitivists, who have informed our understanding of how learning happens, and which is described in the work of cognitive psychologists and learning scientists. LLMs, which are built on neural networks designed around the idea of computer-as-mind, are the mirror of the Cognitivists' conception of mind-as-computer.

Generative learning is a sense-making activity. It involves making sense of learning materials that might be provided by a teacher (or for our purposes, by GAI in the role of an expert) by actively organising and integrating it with one's existing

4.2 Generative Learning

knowledge. Generative learning therefore depends not only on how information is presented to learners (i.e., the instructional methods) but also very much on how learners try to make sense of it (i.e., the learning *strategies* designed or learning *activities* to encourage that sense-making). This process is key: Generative learning is also active learning, inspired by Constructivism, in that it asks learners to engage with knowledge in the form of materials (from a teacher, a text, or the output of GAI) and to integrate that output to construct their own knowledge, so that they can then apply to another context. This process of knowledge construction, which Wittrock called sense-making, is fundamental when working with GAI, to encourage critical thinking, interrogation of its output, to conscious engagement with the process of sense-making.

Generative learning theory is also reflected Mayer's Select-Organise-Integrate (SOI) model of generative learning (Fiorella & Mayer, 2015), where "the processes of organising and integrating are referred to as *generative processing*, which involves building a new mental representation based on one's relevant existing knowledge" (my italics). In the SOI framework, learning also involves three primary cognitive processes: Learners select the incoming sensory information; organise the selected information into a mental representation; and integrate that representation with long-term memory. SOI's select-organise-integrate is very close to Wittrock's original conception of attention (selecting), building internal connections (organising), and building external connections (integrating), and also recognises the role of metacognitive and motivational processes in generative learning.

Generative learning as an approach has been revitalised in recent years through the work of Fiorella and Mayer, who took Wittrock's four original components of sense-making (generation, motivation, attention, memory) and translated them into instructional methods aimed at promoting student understanding. They came up with a series of generative learning strategies to assist with "the process of transforming incoming information (e.g., words and pictures) into usable knowledge (e.g., mental models, schemas)." Their generative learning strategies (Fiorella & Mayer, 2016; Brod, 2020) help students make sense of this output by summarising, mapping, drawing, imagining, self-testing, self-explaining, teaching, and enacting—all generative activities we can imagine engaging in with GAI as a peer or learning partner.

Fiorella (2023) proposed a framework to describe how learners make sense of conceptual learning material, which identifies three sense-making modes that each serve unique and complementary cognitive functions. These are *explaining* (generating coherent verbal representations), *visualising* (generating coherent visual representations) and *enacting* (generating coherent motor representations). Each sense-making mode serves unique and complementary functions: generalising, organising, and simulating one's knowledge. Explaining generalises one's knowledge; visualising organises one's knowledge; and enacting simulates one's knowledge. The primary assumption of this framework is that the visualising and enacting modes serve to facilitate the explaining mode. These three sense-making modes can be used to frame the generative learning strategies (i.e., learning activities) listed above to help scaffold learning and promote sense-making (Table 4.1).

Table 4.1 Sense-making modes, generative processes modes, and generative strategies

Sense-making modes	Explain		Visualise		Enact	
Generative processing modes	Select		Organise		Integrate	
Generative strategies	Summarise	Teach/Test	Map/Draw	Imagine	Explain	Create

Educators can use these generative learning strategies to engage with GAI using the three sense-making modes—asking questions, generating responses, interrogating those responses; generating drawings, images, and concept maps; asking for explanations of difficult concepts, testing one's understanding of that concept, and making predictions based on data. But the critical step in sense-making is metacognitive monitoring, through prior knowledge activation and memory retrieval. This is also where the role of the human teacher is so important, to ensure that the critical metacognitive work is done that enables learners to construct coherent mental representations that enable them to apply their knowledge in new situations.

Ultimately, these categories of sense-making modes or cognitive processes are simply ways of thinking about how to plan learning and design learning activities (or generative learning strategies) that can assist in the larger goal of sense-making. The role of the educator is to take these ideas and transform them into learning experiences that help students make sense of the topic. This metacognitive monitoring is the essential human contribution to the human-and-AI collaboration. Luckin et al. (2024), citing Daniel Kahneman's *Thinking Fast and Slow* (2013), has pointed to the critical role of self-efficacy in shaping our cognitive abilities, arguing that Kahneman's two systems of the human mind provide a valuable framework for exploring this interconnectedness. "According to Kahneman, System 1 is automatic, and outside our voluntary control. It is home to our instincts. It includes innate behaviours and learned associations that can be speeded up through practice. In contrast, System 2 is effortful, within our conscious control, and associated with the kind of complex thinking we typically associate with intelligence." Luckin underlines their interconnectedness: "System 2, our intelligent mind, cannot exist without the foundation provided by System 1, our instinctive mind. This challenges the notion of intelligence as a purely rational, conscious process and highlights the importance of our automatic, unconscious mental processes. It also highlights a key difference between AI and Human Intelligence" (Luckin et al., 2024).

Generative learning puts the process of learning at the forefront, with these human skills at the centre. Regardless of where AI system development leads, GAI's attributes make it ideally suited for constructivist approaches that position generative learning as a sense-making activity. Explanations, visualisation, and enactments are excellent places to start when working with GenAI, the results of which students can engage with and analyse. But without this deliberate focus on critical analysis—on sensemaking—AI can substitute for critical reasoning and thereby reduce student agency to take control of their own learning (Darvishi et al., 2024). It is therefore the role of the educator to invite students to critically engage with its output, to consider and weigh it next to their own preconceived notions, and to arrive at a new place of understanding. Far from limiting students' learning, when used in the context of generative learning's sense-making modes, GAI can be an "engine of engagement" (Stodd et al., 2023).

4.3 Digital Design

We know that learning is not only generative but also a social and iterative process. Indeed, learning is dialogic, which makes chatbots natural partners in learning. They provide a conversational interface for learners to interact with, where natural language processing and understanding is used to analyse and understand language in social interactions, to answer questions, to provide feedback and to engage in dialogue. But designing education that uses GAI as a generative, social, conversational, psychological other possessed of an alien intelligence is no small task. How can we use learning through dialogue with GAI to create active learning that enables to students make sense of their discipline and the world?

Learning design is the pedagogically-grounded practice of designing learning experiences based on evidence-based pedagogy. It emerged from cognitive and behavioural psychology and was initially used to design training. The field grew rapidly as a discipline during the Web 2.0 era, as the growing body of research into the use of learning technologies revealed best practices for the use of technology to support learning. Instructional Design, Educational Development and Learning Science each focus in different ways on how people learn, which inform how digital learning is designed. As education has become a blend of digital and analogue, these design principles and practices are increasingly relevant to all modes of delivery. Indeed, all education is now digital and, as such, all educators should understand these basic design principles and how to implement them in their teaching.

Like TPACK, digital design also combines three key areas of knowledge: disciplinary expertise (content), instructional/learning design (pedagogy), and learning technologies (technology). It is a team-based, collaborative approach to course design, if not delivery, wherein a typical team will include the academic (subject matter expert), a learning designer (the digital pedagogy expert), and a learning technologist (the tools and technologies expert). Each of these roles brings a distinct and equally important set of expertise to the table (Fig. 4.1).

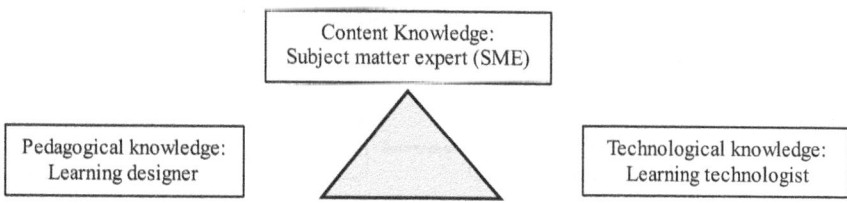

Fig. 4.1 The design team

4.4 Constructive Alignment

There are a number of fundamental principles that guide the work of learning designers but probably none more important than the principle of constructive alignment (Biggs, 1999, 2014) also referred to as backwards design: "Constructive alignment' starts with the notion that the learner constructs his or her own learning through relevant learning activities. The teacher's job is to create a learning environment that supports the learning activities appropriate to achieving the desired learning outcomes. The key is that all components in the teaching system—the curriculum and its intended outcomes, the teaching methods used, the assessment tasks—are aligned to each other. All are tuned to learning activities addressed in the desired learning outcomes. The learner finds it difficult to escape without learning appropriately" (Biggs, 1999). Constructive alignment of the key elements in a course—of learning outcomes, learning activities, learning materials and evaluation of learning—means in practice that the design process starts with the end in mind (i.e., the learning goals) rather than with a list of content or topics to be covered. This alignment of outcomes, assessment, activities and content is a foundational principle in digital learning design because if the core elements are not aligned, the design will not help the learner to meet their goals. In online education, constructive alignment is the gold standard for course design. Indeed, a course that is not constructively aligned will fail the review for digital course design conducted by international quality standards bodies like Quality Matters (Fig. 4.2).

Why is this important in the context of GAI? The knowledge, skills and competencies that students need to master are changing. What do we define as a human competency? What is an AI competency? How can we use AI to teach human competencies—or can we? These are important questions that will determine the shape of learning design in the future. As we have seen from the discussion of TPACK to TPAIK, we need to consider not just AI and human competencies, but also how GAI is changing disciplinary competencies, and use the answer to that question to rethink the courses and programmes we design. This has enormous implications in terms of assessment and accreditation, which is discussed in Chap. 6, but for the purposes of the design of learning activities, it is important to be mindful of this relationship between knowledge, skills and competencies, and the learning activities that we design to support learners in developing them.

Digital technologies can be used to support active learning approaches but, as the above makes clear, thoughtful and purposeful design is required in order to do so effectively. Constructivism and Social Constructivism highlight the importance of active and social learning for the construction of student understanding, where

Fig. 4.2 Constructive alignment (Backwards design)

4.4 Constructive Alignment

the focus shifts from the instructor to the learner. Digital practices combine Connectivism's view of students as agents in the digital network with Constructivism's focus on active learning, where the process is inherently social and depends on interaction with others in the network. How can we design learning that invites students to participate with GAI in this active and social process of sense-making? How can we move beyond the early phase of experimentation to using GAI productively to develop critical and evolving domain expertise?

There are numerous instructional/learning design frameworks to choose from but the best known is the ADDIE model, developed at Florida State University in 1975, which stands for Analyse, Design, Develop, Implement, Evaluate—the five key phases in instructional design. There are many other design models but the most popular include Gagne's 9 Events of Instruction, which organises the learning process into a 9-stage process; the Successive Approximation Model (SAM), which was developed as an alternative to ADDIE; Merrill's First Principles of Instruction, which names the universal principles that are common to all effective design models (task-centred; activation; demonstration; application; integration); and the Dick and Carey Model, also known as the Systems Approach Model, which assumes that all of the elements in a learning experience form an interrelated system (instructor, students, instructional materials and activities, teaching techniques and the learning environment) that defines the outcome.

The most famous framework of all, of course, is Bloom's Taxonomy (Bloom et al., 1956; Gogus, 2012) and the ubiquitous pyramid that all educators recognise. Bloom's is not so much a learning design framework as a representation of the stages of development in the three key learning domains: cognitive, affective, and psychomotor. The cognitive domain is focused on intellectual skills like critical thinking and the pyramid showing the cognitive hierarchy is the one most often shared. Bloom's stages of development (originally listed as knowledge, comprehension, application, analysis, synthesis, evaluation) helps educators to design learning that scaffolds this cognitive development as part of the learning experience they design. How might that process unfold when learner is engaging with a conversational GAI expert? What is the process by which we hone these intellectual skills? What learning activities do we need to design to develop them? Learning design plays a critical role here.

The affective domain has not historically received the same attention as the cognitive but it is very important for student motivation and engagement—and has the potential to be just as important in the AI age, given the social and conversational affordances of GAI. The affective domain focuses on the attitude, values and interests of learners, and the hierarchy (receiving, responding, valuing, organisation, characterisation) focuses on helping learners to understand how they develop these values. Finally, the psychomotor domain, based on Harrow's taxonomy of the psychomotor domain (Harrow, 1972) represents the learner's ability to perform physical movements and tasks, and here the hierarchy (reflex, basic movements, perceptual abilities, physical abilities, skilled movements, non-discursive communication) ranges from basic movements to expression through physical activity. Robots are now part of the GAI ecosystem and advances in health and medicine in particular suggest that Bloom's scaffolding of a learner's abilities to perform physical tasks could be applied to machines.

Table 4.2 Bloom's 4.0

Bloom's 1.0 (1956)	Bloom's 2.0 (2001)	+ AI	Bloom's 4.0 (2024)
Synthesis	Create		Recommendation + action
Evaluation	Evaluate		Evaluation + feedback
Analysis	Analyse		Case study + critique
Application	Apply		Scenario + role
Comprehension	Understand		Explanation + feedback
Knowledge	Remember		Information + examples

4.5 Bloom's 2.0 to 4.0

Bloom's taxonomy was revised in 2001 for the digital age, when the original nouns were replaced with active verbs (remember, understand, apply, analyse, evaluate, create). This update reflected the shift in the role of the instructor from sage-on-the-stage to guide-on-the-side, and from the view of the student as passive receiver of information to the learner as active participant and agent in the construction of their own learning (Anderson & Krathwohl, 2001). Bloom's now needs to be updated again to consider how learners interact with AI. What is the value of remembering in a world where GAI can summon up all the information that exists in a millisecond? How does our capacity for understanding need to change when GAI can explain everything to us, for us and often better than us? How should we analyse information when AI can help us to do it more efficiently and effectively? How do we apply the information generated by and with GenAI? How do we evaluate GenAI output created alongside human experts? A new Bloom's is required that reflects the collaboration that lies at the heart of the new hybrid of human + AI, that reflects the new ways of knowing and learning. From creating knowledge and understanding; to assisting with the process of analysing and evaluating; to making recommendations and suggesting actions, collaboration with AI forms the heart of it. Blooms 4.0 reflects this collaboration by replacing the active verb with the actions that GAI takes and the resources it generates for learning (Table 4.2).

4.6 Generativism

But what does this mean in practice? How do we collaborate with GAI to design learning? Generativism describes the symbiotic approach to designing and delivering learning in collaboration with GAI. It is grounded in the principle of learning as a process and is informed by some of the most important and influential learning theories and approaches of our age: Constructivism, which highlights the need for active learning to construct meaning; Connectivism, which stresses the role of the digital network in which students are active agents in that learning; Social Learning, which stresses the importance of the community and collaboration; Experiential Learning, which highlights the role of learning by doing and reflecting on that experience; and Generative Learning, which presents learning as a sense-making process using schemata.

Co-design and delivery with GAI is the defining feature of generativism as a practice, whereby knowledge is generated by working in collaboration with GAI, through learning activities that are codesigned with, facilitated by, and assessed with GAI. It can be summarised as: (1) codesign of the learning experience in collaboration with GAI; (2) codelivery of the learning activities and assessments in collaboration with GAI; and (3) assessment of learning as a process in collaboration with GAI.

Generativism uses established digital frameworks as the foundation, which provide the methodological approach we need to navigate this new terrain of designing learning in and for GAI-mediated environments. Based on conversation, connection, community and collaboration, they are natural fits for GAI's generative and social affordances. By starting with these trusted digital frameworks, we can rethink course and programme designs for the age of GAI with a focus on active, social, collaborative and constructivist approaches that address the critical need for AI competencies but as part of a holistic experience that is human-centred, community-oriented and student-focused.

4.7 Learning as Dialogue

Laurillard created the Conversational Framework (2002, 2012) to emphasise the role of interaction and collaboration in creating understanding. She wanted to encourage educators to think about the learning experience from the student's point of view, as opposed to their own. We can see in these ideas similar themes to those that Eric Mazur was exploring when he used peer instruction in his flipped classroom at Harvard in the late 1990s. Just as generative learning theory draws on the work of the earlier cognitive theorists, Laurillard's framework is also distillation of ideas drawn from the key learning theories, which she reduced to four key elements: instructionism, social learning, constructionism, and collaborative learning.

According to the Conversational Framework, learning is an activity that takes place informally throughout our lives. We develop a concept, act upon it, and modify the concept based on the feedback we receive on that action. Learning therefore takes place through a process of action, reflection, feedback and clarification loops. But this process of developing and integrating concepts and practices happens through *interaction* with educators and peers, who give us feedback. It is therefore a social and constructive process, whereby educators and learners model and share practice through their actions and feedback within a learning environment. With each interaction—or loop—between learners and educators, and learners and their peers, there is an opportunity for learning and improvement.

Here we can again detect the influence of cognitive psychology and neuroscience in idea of the learning process as taking place through iterative sequences of feedback

Table 4.3 The six learning activity types map (roughly) to generative learning strategies

Generative strategies	Teach/Test	Summarise	Explain	Imagine	Map/Draw	Create
Learning activities	Acquisition	Investigation	Discussion	Collaboration	Practice	Production

and clarification loops, which remind us of Mayer's "generative processing" and Wittrock's "schemata." Whether it is the generative process of sense-making through generative learning activities or the conception of learning as generative processing, these frameworks and approaches are all ultimately concerned with sense-making through active learning (Table 4.3).

The Conversational Framework is a natural partner for the design of active learning with conversational AI because it allows educators to use GAI as a dialogic partner. This transforms formerly passive learning (reading a book or article, watching a video, listening to a podcast) into an active learning activity because the student can interrogate the source as they read/watch/listen. This level of interactivity has the potential to deepen learning, making it a personal experience in which the student can speak directly to the expert in the source, asking their own questions of it—by having a conversation with it. GAI amplifies the experience by personalising it and augmenting the individual's ability to perform these tasks.

4.8 Active Generative Learning

In 2015, digital practitioners at University College London took Laurillard's Conversational Framework and used it as the basis for a framework for the rapid conversion of face-to-face learning to online delivery. The result of this effort was the ABC Learning Design Framework (abc-ld.org), in which the ABC acronym stands for Arena, Blended Connected, which refers to UCL's Arena faculty development programme; blended learning; and the connected curriculum (Gramp, 2020). In ABC workshops, participants think about how teaching is delivered in the classroom using various learning activity types and then use the framework to convert these activities into a digital format. This approach has been widely adopted to create fully online and blended learning courses and programmes. This methodology is very useful as a starting point from which to consider how design learning with GAI using Laurillard's learning activity types.

ABC begins with a workshop, during which educators map out the ways that they currently deliver their lessons, using colour-coded cards to identify the learning activity types. These are Acquisition, Investigation, Discussion, Collaboration, Discussion, Production and Practice. Of these, only the first—Acquisition—is passive, in the sense that it involves the learner taking in information from a source, be that a teacher, a lecture, a video or a book. The other five are active learning activities that require the learner to engage in the process of constructing their understanding of a concept through practice. Together, the six learning activity types cover every type of learning activity a student is likely to encounter, and together they make up the entire conversational framework. Classroom learning activities are categorised according to activity type, which is the starting point from which to design activities using digital tools that accomplish the same learning goals.

Taking analogue classroom learning activities and transforming them for digital delivery will often mean that, as per the SAMR framework, a certain activity is no longer usable and need to be completely designed. The TPACK framework is also implicit in this process, as participants need to bring their content, pedagogical and technological knowledge to bear on the exercise. For educators who are new to digital learning, the ABC workshop can be an eye-opener in terms of helping them to analyse their own educational practice and reconceive of it for delivery in digital spaces. For many, it is their first formal interaction with instructional design and concepts like constructive alignment and report that it has a positive knock-on impact on their classroom lesson design. For educators keen to integrate GAI but without much experience in digital design, the ABC framework is an ideal starting point.

With generative learning theory's sense-making/processing modes and generative strategies in mind, educators can use Laurillard's Conversational Framework to guide their thinking about how to create learning in dialogue with GAI. Then, using the ABC learning design framework and the guidance on the new hybrid from Chap. 2, they can design learning activities with and for GAI. The original ABC framework was created for the Web 2.0 era, so the types of activities originally envisioned were products of that age. This means that, as per SAMR, they will need to be modified or redefined but thinking through that process can help educators to imagine how to integrate and use GAI in their teaching. Below, we present each of the original six ABC learning activity types and briefly suggest how they could be used with GAI, without being overly prescriptive about the activity that instructors might design.

4.8.1 Acquisition

Acquisition was originally defined as a relatively passive learning activity type: "Learning through acquisition is what learners are doing when they are listening to a lecture or a podcast, reading from books or websites." But when designing learning activities with GAI, such learning has the potential to become much more active and indeed, more interactive, with conversational AI. From interactive textbooks to YouTube videos to custom GPTs, educators can build custom resources to bring formerly static content to life. Custom GPTs using textbooks as the source for RAG, a NotebookLM containing a variety of documents, or simply uploading a book or document to Claude will allow learners to ask questions about the information.

4.8.2 Investigation

In the original ABC Learning Design framework, "Learning through investigation guides the learner to explore, compare and critique the texts, documents and resources that reflect the concepts and ideas being taught." But every aspect of learning is changing with GAI and learners engaged in investigation—or research—now have many options. Perplexity is disrupting the entire category of internet search and research-specific tools like Elicit, Semantic Search and Scite allow learners and students to search in targeted and sophisticated ways, and that research and investigation is an activity done in collaboration with GAI.

4.8.3 Discussion

The ABC Learning Design framework says that "learning through discussion requires the learner to articulate their ideas and questions, and to challenge and respond to the ideas from the teacher, and/or from their peers." We have focused on Laurillard's Conversational Framework here but it would be useful to draw in other theories such as Bakhtin's theory of dialogism (Holquist, 2002) to look at dialogism with GAI using discussion with AI avatars and characters, which might be experts, moderators or peers. These discussions might use a platforms like Circle Chat designed for group chat with AI avatars, or the custom bots discussed in Chap. 3 to engage in a group human + AI discussion.

4.8.4 Collaboration

The ABC Learning Design framework says that "learning through collaboration embraces main discussion, practice and production. Building on investigations and acquisition, it is about taking part in the process of knowledge building itself." Generativism is based on the idea of collaboration with GAI in every type of learning activity, so this underpins the entire approach of designing learning activities with GAI. Chapter 5 is focused on personalised learning within a social community and focuses on how to design a learning experience that incorporates multiples presences—human and AI—into such an environment.

4.8.5 Practice

In ABC, "Learning through practice enables the learner to adapt their actions to the task goal, and use the feedback to improve their next action. Feedback may come from self-reflection, from peers, from the teacher or from the activity itself, if it shows them how to improve the result of their action in relation to the goal." GAI allows learners to practice and get feedback instantly. For example, students can practice conversational skills in other languages with tools like Lang AI or use AI-powered writing tools to generate or co-write, before critiquing the output and reflecting on the experience. Practice is changing in all disciplines, so it is important to revisit the disciplinary skills and competencies before designing any activities.

4.8.6 Production

In the ABC Learning Design framework, "learning through production is the way the teacher motivates the learner to consolidate what they have learned by articulating their current conceptual understanding and how they used it in practice." Production using text and image generation is where the vast majority of the conversation on GAI tools focused initially. But there are now many examples of educators incorporating GAI into their classes and using the comparison of AI versus human output as a starting point for discussion. From writing to music to video production, the creative disciplines are now using AI to create products, so engagement with this shift will be key. Students can, for example, generate music and video with GAI and analyse the output using those generative learning strategies for sense-making.

Learning activity	ABC	+ GenAI
Acquisition	Learning through acquisition is what learners are doing when they are listening to a lecture or a podcast, reading from books or websites	Research tools + data analysis with chatbots, private LLMs, agents
Collaboration	Learning through collaboration embraces discussion, practice and production. Building on investigations and acquisition, it is about taking part in the process of knowledge building itself	Collaboration with AI assistants, tutors, buddies + guides
Discussion	Learning through discussion requires the learner to articulate their ideas and questions, and to challenge and respond to the ideas from the teacher, and/or from their peers	Discussion with AI characters, experts + moderators
Investigation	Learning through investigation guides the learner to explore, compare and critique the texts, documents and resources that reflect the concepts and ideas being taught	Investigation using chatbot output + student critique + data analysis

(continued)

(continued)

Learning activity	ABC	+ GenAI
Practice	Learning through practice enables the learner to adapt their actions to the task goal, and use the feedback to improve their next action. Feedback may come from self-reflection, from peers, the teacher or the activity itself, if it shows how to improve the result of their action in relation to the goal	Discipline-specific GAI tools and/or chatbot output + personal feedback, testing + iterating
Production	Learning through production is the way the teacher motivates the learner to consolidate what they have learned by articulating their current conceptual understanding and how they used it in practice	Generation of synthetic resources + iterative prompt engineering as learning

There are many examples from innovators and practitioners, who have been testing AI in their classes and sharing their practice. The most high profile are the Wharton School's Ethan and Lilach Mollick, who have together published several papers (Mollick & Mollick, 2022, 2023, 2024). There are also several hundred examples from lesser known educators who experiment, test and share their work in online groups and webinars. Several collections of these experiments have been published, along with reflections, which are valuable starting points for any educator just beginning to dip their toe into these waters. These include Nerantzi et al's (2023) crowd-sourced collection of *101 Creative Ideas to use AI in Education* and the follow-up edition (2024); Harvard Metalab AI Pedagogy Project's growing collection of lesson plans; and Buyserie and Thurston's (2024) *Teaching and generative AI: Pedagogical possibilities and productive tensions*, which provides first-person accounts of educators' experiences. These are just one small sample of the resources that innovative educators have created and shared, so that others can start to integrate GAI intentionally into their teaching.

Learning is a generative activity and Education 4.0 does not mean using technology to reinforce outmoded ways of teaching and learning. The innovation we have seen in digital education over the last two decades risks being undermined if we use GAI to revert to outdated models of delivery. GAI, rather than increasing automation in education, should enable more interaction, more active learning, more personalisation. The focus for educators therefore needs to be on the design of active, collaborative and constructivist learning that encourages sense-making and critical engagement rather than the generation of content. AI pedagogy is emerging and it is clear that the future of education lies in codesign with GAI. International organisations have begun the work of creating frameworks for GAI integration (Miao & Holmes, 2023; Miao & Tawil, 2024) but there has been very little discussion of how to actually integrate co-design into education. Generativism uses frameworks from the digital era as the foundation with which to construct something new, offering an approach to designing and delivering learning experiences that are social, collaborative, community-oriented and human-centred. In the next chapter, we turn to GAI's social affordances and explore the potential to create personalised and peer learning.

References

Anderson, L., & Krathwohl, D. A. (2001). *Taxonomy for learning, teaching and assessing: A revision of Bloom's taxonomy of educational objectives*. Longman.

Biggs, J. (1999). What the student does: Teaching for enhanced learning. *Higher Education Research & Development, 18*(1), 57–75. https://doi.org/10.1080/0729436990180105

Biggs, J. (2014). Constructive alignment in university teaching. *HERDSA Review of Higher Education, 1*, 5–22.

Bloom, B. S., Engelhart, M. D., Furst, E. J., Hill, W. H., & Krathwohl, D. R. (1956). *Taxonomy of educational objectives: The classification of educational goals by a committee of college and university examiners (Handbook I: Cognitive domain)*. Longmans Publishing.

Brod, G. (2020). Generative learning: Which strategies for what age? *Educational Psychology Review, 2021*(33), 1295–1318. https://doi.org/10.1007/s10648-020-09571-9

Buyserie, B., & Thurston, T. N. (Eds.) (2024). *Teaching and generative AI: Pedagogical possibilities and productive tensions*. Utah State University.

Darvishi, A., Khosravi, H., Sadiq, S., Gašević, D., & Siemens, G. (2024). Impact of AI assistance on student agency. *Computers and Education, 210*, March 2024. https://doi.org/10.1016/j.compedu.2023.104967

Fiorella, L. (2023). Making sense of generative learning. *Educational Psychology Review, 35*, 50. https://doi.org/10.1007/s10648-023-09769-7

Fiorella, L., & Mayer, R. E. (2015). *Learning as a generative activity: Eight learning strategies that promote understanding*. Cambridge University Press. https://doi.org/10.1017/CBO9781107707085

Fiorella, L., & Mayer, R. E. (2016). Eight ways to promote generative learning. *Educational Psychology Review, 28*, 717–741. https://doi.org/10.1007/s10648-015-9348-9

Gogus, A. (2012). Bloom's taxonomy of learning objectives. In N. M. Seel (Eds.), *Encyclopedia of the sciences of learning*. Springer. https://doi.org/10.1007/978-1-4419-1428-6_141

Gramp, J. (2020). ABC LD workshop localisation. https://abc-ld.org/wp-content/uploads/2020/05/01-ABC_LD-Toolkit-Intro-Erasmus-v02.pdf

Harrow, A. J. (1972). *A taxonomy of the psychomotor domain*. David McKay Co.

Holquist, M. (2002). *Dialogism: Bakhtin and his world*. Routledge.

Kahneman, D. (2013). *Thinking, fast and slow*. Farrar, Straus and Giroux.

Laurillard, D. (2002). *Rethinking university teaching: A conversational framework for the effective use of learning technologies* (2nd ed.). Routledge. https://doi.org/10.4324/9781315012940

Laurillard, D. (2012). *Teaching as a design science: Building pedagogical patterns for learning and technology*. Routledge. https://doi.org/10.4324/9780203125083

Luckin, R., et al. (2024, June). Exploring the future of learning and the relationship between human intelligence and AI. An interview with Professor Rose Luckin. *Journal of Applied Learning & Teaching, 7*(1).

Miao, F., & Holmes, W. (2023). *Guidance for generative AI in education and research*. UNESCO 2023. ISBN 978-92-3-100612-8.

Miao, F., & Tawil, S. (2024). Steering the digital transformation of education: UNESCO's human-centered approach. *Frontiers of Digital Education, 1*(1), 51–58. https://doi.org/10.3868/s110-009-024-0005-6

Mollick, E., & Mollick, L. (2022, December 13). New modes of learning enabled by AI chatbots: Three methods and assignments. https://doi.org/10.2139/ssrn.4300783

Mollick, E. R., & Mollick, L. (2023). Assigning AI: Seven approaches for students, with prompts. https://doi.org/10.2139/ssrn.4475995

Mollick, E. R., & Mollick, L. (2024). Instructors as innovators: A future-focused approach to new AI learning opportunities, with prompts. https://doi.org/10.2139/ssrn.4802463

Nerantzi, C., Abegglen, S., Karatsiori, M., & Martínez-Arboleda, A. (Eds.). (2023). *101 creative ideas to use AI in education, A crowdsourced collection* (2023 1.0) [Computer software]. Zenodo. https://doi.org/10.5281/zenodo.8072950

Stodd, J., Schatz, S., & Stead, G. (2023). *Engines of engagement: A curious book about generative AI*. Sea Salt Publishing. https://seasaltlearning.com/engines-of-engagement-generative-ai-book/

Wittrock, M. C. (1974). Learning as a generative process. *Educational Psychologist, 11*, 87–95.

Wittrock, M. C. (1989). Educational psychology and the future of research in learning, instruction, and teaching. In M. C. Wittrock & F. Farley (Eds.), *The future of educational psychology* (pp. 75–89). Lawrence Erlbaum Associates, Inc.

Chapter 5
Intelligent Communities

Abstract This chapter explores the implications of generative learning design for personalised and peer learning. It begins with a discussion of personalised learning via adaptive learning and intelligent tutor systems, before looking at GAI tutors and moving to a discussion about social learning and digital communities. It suggests using digital frameworks to design collaborative, inquiry-based learning that capitalises on the social affordances of GAI to create inquiry-based, human-centred learning for the AI age.

Keywords Community · Personalised learning · Intelligent tutoring systems (ITS) · Adaptive learning platforms · Bots and tutors · Social learning · Affective computing · Inquiry-based learning · Community of Inquiry (CoI)

5.1 Introduction

GAI is hyper-personalising all of our digital experiences, as the algorithms that track our online activity are increasingly able to target our wants and desires. One day in the not too distant future, we might watch a series on Netflix or a video on YouTube that is generated just for us, based on our own personal preferences. This is not the stuff of the sci-fi future but already here. Perplexity hosts a daily AI-generated podcast called Discovery Daily, which is narrated by "Alex," an Eleven Labs-generated voice. Musicians are releasing tracks made with AI. Actors are licensing the use of their voice and likeness for commercial production. Content that was traditionally created by experts alone is being replaced by content that is AI-generated and co-created. Hyper-personalisation is replacing mass consumption, such that soon every user will soon enjoy their own, unique experience. These shifts towards hyper-personalisation and co-creation with AI have significant implications for education.

GAI offers the long-awaited solution to Bloom's 2 Sigma problem, that true mastery of a topic requires 1:1 tutoring (Bloom, 1984). Scalable personalised learning is now possible with AI-powered systems using learner analytics. GAI assistants and tutors can remember all of the information on an individual, allowing learners to have extended conversations on any topic. They also learn from experience, which means they can serve as a personal tutor in any field. With RAG, educators can create customised tutors for their own specific purposes. This is the hyper-personalisation of user experiences for education, where every educator now has the potential to be an innovator (Mollick & Mollick, 2024). With this, the role of the educator in the learning community is also shifting, from solo expert in the room to co-facilitator in a digital space shared with multiple intelligences.

Learning is also social and learners do better when they feel a sense of belonging to a community. Future skills include not just critical thinking, creativity and resilience but also teamwork and collaboration, which social and inquiry-based learning can help develop. GAI is also social, interacting with users as a presence. These social affordances allow us to connect the personal to the peer, to create connections and foster community using student-centred approaches like inquiry-based learning. But leveraging GAI in communities of learning requires added care to ensure that student wellbeing is protected. Designing for such a learning community requires thoughtful and intentional approaches grounded in best practice. Frameworks from digital education provide the foundations with which to design of social, collaborative, community-oriented and inquiry-based learning that leverages GAI, combining personalised and peer learning, and enables us to design and create educational experiences that are AI-powered but human-centred.

5.2 Intelligent Tutoring Systems

Personalised (or adaptive) learning originated from 1960s research into intelligent tutoring systems (ITS) driven by AI. These are computerised learning environments that incorporate computational models from the cognitive sciences, learning sciences, computational linguistics, AI, mathematics, and other fields (Luckin et al., 2016), propelled by research like Sleeman and Brown's (1982) early book *Intelligent Tutoring Systems*, which included contributors from AI, cognitive science and education (Guo et al., 2021). The system creates a model of the student's knowledge—a digital profile—and uses this to provide a personal tutor (Chassignol et al., 2018), which curates content and provides feedback and hints to help answer questions, then uses the data collected from student interactions to make recommendations and provide personalised pathways (Bates, 2019, p. 593). Of course, classroom teachers have always been able to create personalised lesson plans for their students but it is extremely labour-intensive, so personalised learning at scale could be transformative for the many who do not have access to high-quality personal instruction.

Historically, these systems were narrow in scape and time-consuming to create. Expert systems relied on a specific data set to give answers, working as assistants and answering questions based on the set of knowledge they were trained on. Most of the AI applications for education focused on content presentation and testing for comprehension, using models of learning based on how computers or computer networks work. These models were generally designed by computer scientists, which meant they also adopted a behaviourist model of learning: present, test, feedback. Until very recently, the objection that "very few so-called AI applications in teaching and learning meet the criteria of massive data, massive computing power and powerful and relevant algorithms" (Bates, 2019) to be useful for education was accurate. But ITS can now facilitate collaboration between learners by providing automated feedback and generating questions for discussion. Proponents argue that they improve interactions between teachers and students by using the information gathered to diagnose differences between students and using it to recommend customised resources. They also argue that by distributing content and teaching materials, ITS can also cut down on some of the work that teachers currently do (Gentile et al., 2023).

5.3 Adaptive Learning Platforms

Like ITS, adaptive learning platforms use data analytics and AI to customise the learning journey for each student by personalising the content, pace and difficulty level. Adaptive learning also involves tracking student progress, engagement, and performance, and providing feedback based on the student's responses and redirecting them based on their performance (Bates, 2019, p. 450). In theory, they allow educators to improve and adjust their courses to better meet the needs of their students, by generating feedback, providing personalised resources, and tailoring activities to students. The attraction of such systems for a sector so bogged down in administrative work is obvious. Such products, not unlike AI-powered custom courseware, offer the convenience of not having to build internally, but come at a cost. There is a wide range of adaptive learning platforms, all of which use AI to offer ready-made and adaptable content. However, most of the LMS systems already used in education already offer some adaptive learning capabilities but to leverage this functionality, the learning content needs to be on the platform, ready for learners to engage with. This requires a blended approach to delivery that uses the LMS as a space for interaction and exchange, rather than as a digital repository.

ITS and adaptive learning platforms rely on learning analytics to work, so these systems require that the technology be connected to the individual student's activities. Privacy preferences vary widely based on geography, cultural norms, political systems and ethical standards. In the UK, for example, CCTV is widely used on the streets and people are not unused to being watched but the understanding is that this surveillance is in the interests of public safety. Being tracked and monitored in education is a different matter. These issues form an important part of the ongoing discussion on AI and its wider adoption in our societies. The EU AI Act has set the international bar for regulation high by classifying all use of AI tools in education as high-risk (European Commission, 2024). As individual users, we also have the power to adjust the settings on the tools we use, such as opting out of a chatbot saving our prompt history or choosing to use tools and platforms that do not store personal information. Having the information and knowing what to choose is an important part of being AI literate.

5.4 Integrated Assistants and Tutors

The first virtual cognitive assistant was Jill Watson, launched in 2016 at Georgia Tech, which was developed to handle the high number of forum posts by students enrolled in an online course required for the school's online master of science in computer science programme. Jill Watson engaged with students in "extended conversations about courseware including textbooks, video transcripts, presentation slides, class syllabi, and other course materials." The initial version used IBM's Watson platform and used the course syllabi to answer student questions posted in online discussion fora. The next version, launched in 2019, switched to Google's BERT as the platform "because it was open-source software and thus could be tuned for Jill" (Goel et al., 2024). The latest version of Jill uses ChatGPT to answer student questions about course materials and to "enhance cognitive engagement and teaching presence." Jill Watson uses RAG to reduce the known issues in GPT by creating prompts for ChatGPT and postprocessing its responses. It also uses a variation on RAG based on the courseware, which researchers have found that this both improves the accuracy and precision in Jill's responses and also reduces hallucinations (Goel et al., 2024).

Institutions are now developing assistants that work more like tutors than assistants. In March 2023, the University of London partnered with Noodle Factory to create an AI Teaching Assistant to "support our online learners with their academic questions." (Armstrong, 2023). Teaching material is uploaded, which the software uses to generate answers to student questions, create and mark assessments, recommend lesson plans and help with grading exam papers—in short, all of the tasks a TA would do. Students can ask questions and receive answer that are "contextualised tutoring, based on meticulously curated information." It would be difficult to see how such a tutor could not at some point take the place of an actual human teaching assistant but it is not unusual to have high enrollment in online courses, where an AI tutor can be a great help.

Tutors are slightly different from AI assistants—while assistants are designed to help with efficiency, tutors are intended to interact on a pedagogical level and improve teaching effectiveness. There is a growing selection of customised tutors, which can be integrated into an LMS or used by learners as a standalone. In March 2023, the Khan Academy announced they would be using GPT-4 to power their new 'Khanmigo' personal tutor. The name was a piece of marketing genius—taking the Spanish phrase "con migo" ("with me") but adapting it for use with the company name to describe a personal tutor to accompany the student throughout their learning experience. It was greeted with enthusiasm and a lot of media attention but received mixed reviews from those who tested it. Later that year, Instructure announced the integration of Khanmigo into its Canvas LMS. Thus the integration of GAI played out very differently with two LMS giants: Anthology's Blackboard created the AI Design Assistant, targeting lecturers lacking the time to create their own online materials, while Instructure's Canvas targets students in need of personalised tutoring. Time will tell which was the best strategic decision for the company but it poses something of a dilemma for educators, in that institutions accessing GAI through an LMS platform will have their GAI capabilities limited to an extent by their institution's choice of LMS.

In fully online environments such as MOOCs, the situation is completely different from traditional face-to-face learning, as the data needed for AI to work is readily available from students interacting with the content and each other on the platform. Here, the potential for online tutors to vastly improve the student experience is clear. This potential was illustrated in a paper published by a group including Yoshua Bengio in 2023, which forecasted a transformation in online learning with an ITS called Korbit designed for use in online machine learning and data science education (St-Hilare et al., 2023). In a comparative study of a traditional MOOC platform delivering content using lecture videos and MCQs and the Korbit platform using personalised and active learning, the results showed "a statistically significant increase in learning outcomes," demonstrating "the tremendous impact that can be achieved with a personalized, active learning AI-powered system." Korbit was a co-author on the study, so a degree of caution is required but the results are impressive, showing dramatic improvements in learning transfer with the use personalised tutors on the platform and demonstrating the potential for AI-powered tutoring in online environments.

The AI-readiness of online environments means that learning analytics can be used to personalise the experience in a way that is not possible otherwise. To make the most of integrated online tutoring, learning content must be on the system and students must interact with it and each other. This is already the case for fully online courses but is significant hurdle for face-to-face institutions unaccustomed to using the LMS as a site for social interaction. This challenge is one that needs to be addressed is GAI is to be usefully integrated into campus-based education. Time will tell whether or not the increasing interest in blended learning encourages wider adoption of AI tutors in on-campus environments or if AI tutors spur an increased interest in blended delivery. The most likely outcome is that AI will drive both upward in the coming years.

5.5 Standalone Assistants and Tutors

There is an understandable appetite to hand off some of the heavy administrative burden many educators bear to AI, as we have seen in the discussion on resource generators. With GAI tutors, AI is moving from administrative efficiency into teaching. What are the implications of this shift? In many institutions, TAs and tutors do much of the grunt work—answering student questions, moderating discussion fora, and often a lot of the grading. But that grunt work is also training to be an educator. When we look these activities from the perspective of generative learning, they are critical in terms of contributing to the process of sense-making. Where lies the line between efficiency and effectiveness? What is being lost in terms of teaching effectiveness when we assume that work like this can be made more efficient with AI? Conversely, what might be gained when an AI takes over the work of a TA?

In 2019, Tony Bates said, "it is difficult to see how 'modern AI' could be used within the current education system, where class sizes or even whole academic departments, and hence data points, are relatively small, in terms of the number needed" (Bates, 2019). There is now another way—the standalone and custom tutor, which exists outside of the institution and is not part of a "solution" for purchase. Instead, these are tutors that educators can use and/or create and customise for their own purposes, with any number of students, anywhere they have access to a device. With models small enough to download and used on a smartphone without an internet connection, the individual instructor now literally has the power in their hands to create whatever sort of learning activities they choose.

For those who prefer to access and use a readymade assistant or tutor that is not affiliated with any institution or corporation, Canadian non-profit Contact North has two standalone tutors—AI Teaching Assistant and an AI Tutor—that are free for anyone to use as they are.

Teaching Assistant Pro, billed as a prototype app, offers to "reduce your workload" and "enhance your teaching" with a "personal teaching assistant to help you with any topic or subject!" and users have the choice of generating multiple choice questions, essay questions and a scoring rubric, or a syllabus, which includes a course description, learning outcomes, an outline, notes and slides. In March 2024, the Syllabot was added, "an AI bot designed to tutor students on a course syllabus." The onus is on the user to craft a prompt that yields good results, as there is no option to upload material or direct the bot to a source of expertise by using RAG.

The second tool, AI Tutor Pro, offers learners the option to upload a document of up to 2200 words (15,000 characters) about which they can then ask the AI tutor questions to "check or grow their knowledge and skills". This allows users to use RAG to help the system better understand a given topic and thereby better help them. In this context, we can see how RAG expands the capabilities of an AI bot from previous expert systems, which were trained to answer questions on a specific data set. Now users can decide what that specific data set is and add it themselves, which empowers the user. In March 2024, a 'Beat the AI' feature was added, which is a self-test game that allows students to team up with a classmate to try outwit the bot and can be played either online or in the classroom. This adds gamification to the tool to help ease the transition from solitary user on the platform to a more social use in the context of a classroom environment. AI Tutor Pro has also been vetted for use by the University of Toronto, which deemed it safe according to their security standards.

Tutello, described as a "human + AI on-demand tutoring platform," uses a combination of AI-generated tutoring with real-life humans that are, as the description suggests, on call for students when needed—but with the delay one would expect of a living being. With the tag line, "every chat has its limits" the idea is that students can access AI-generated advice anytime but can also flag a question for a human tutor to follow up on during office hours. Essentially, the platform offers a combination of help-yourself AI tutoring with the more familiar online office hours approach. Striking the balance between human and AI is clearly the goal but the challenge for Tutello will likely be to figuring out how to scale the humans.

Finally, the UK-based Cottesmore School partnered with Interactive Tutor to conduct a build-your- own-bot project, where senior girls and boys created their own AI versions of faculty. In a LinkedIn post, Tom Rogerson talked about the motivation behind the project: "AI is here to stay and we have a duty to explain it to each other and to young people who will have to exist with it in the future in a much more profound way than presently" (Rogerson, 2024). He explained that the point of the project was for students to hone "skills surrounding prompts, language, design, information architecture and ontology" and said students were "using their own work, they are looking metacognitively into learning, teaching, knowledge and human connection." Students created several bots, including the cleverly named Ptolemai for geography; Railey for arts; Fibonaicci for maths; Faize for sciences; Mairie for languages; and Plaito for philosophy.

The potential opportunities of AI tutors often leads fears that these systems can completely replace the figure of the educators; indeed, Selwyn has written at length about the potential for robots to replace teachers (Selwyn, 2019). Gentile et al. argue that "the human factor is an irreplaceable characteristic of the teacher. The teacher is a guide and reference for students' growth and a compass for their ethical and moral development. In this sense, these tools, which are first glance seem antagonistic to the teacher, are facilitators of the quality interactions that characterise the teaching process" (Gentile et al., 2023). Still, there is no denying that the relationship between the educator and the student is inevitably altered by the introduction of a third (or fourth, or fifth), possibly competing, presence onto the scene.

How does this impact the learning experience? Students certainly benefit in terms of getting a quick answer on coursework or an assignment but they will lose out on the human experience the human TA or tutor brings. Equally, the TA or tutor also misses out on the valuable professional experience that comes with filling such a role, which is all too often the closest to teacher training a Ph.D. student might get before becoming a lecturer. What do we risk losing when this relationship is taken over by AI and educators-in-waiting lose out on this on-the-job learning? Is this not the apprenticeship we advocate for in all other professions in the form of authentic learning experience? If we offload such work to AI, we need to be cognisant of the implications of this trade-off in the longer-term and be prepared to train future educators in and for a very different landscape. We also need to prepare for the changes that the introduction of multiple alien presences as experts or peers into the learning community will bring to the educator-student relationship and to the learning community.

5.6 Social Learning

Individuals can learn alone using personalised tutors and on adaptive learning platforms but students also exist in the physical world, where it is normal to learn with peers and in communities. Sense-making activity does not only happen in isolation, it also happens within social spaces. Social learning frames learning as the construction and sharing of that 'meaning' within and between individuals and across organisations. Indeed, the social space is often where sense-making happens, in collaboration with peers and mentors. "Learning is an intensely human activity, that benefits enormously from personal relationships and social interaction. This relational aspect of learning can be handled equally well online as face-to-face, but it means using computing to support communication." (Bates, 2019, p. 604) The emotional and social aspect of learning—Bloom's affective domain—is just as important as the cognitive. Students who feel like they belong are more likely to attend class and interact with peers than those who do not, and belonging to a community makes for better academic outcomes. In fully online learning environments, community building is purposefully designed to ensure that the isolation that students endured during the Covid pandemic is not their experience. Educators working at institutions with less experience in digital environments need to be cognisant of the need to design this part of the learning experience. The so-called "edtech tragedy" (West, 2023) of the pandemic should never be repeated, so for institutions adopting more digital approaches this means that community must be purposefully designed.

Connection between learners is critical. Connectivism, aside from seeing students as nodes in a network, also promotes learning outside of an individual and in the digital ecosystem, where any person or object can be connected to another. It promotes collaboration and discussion, allowing for different viewpoints and perspectives when it comes to decision-making, problem-solving, and making sense-making. It supports the diversity of opinions and disputes the idea of a hierarchy in the value of knowledge. Stodd et al. have commented that "Meaning-making goes beyond the transfer of information, the production of knowledge, and even the individual—becoming an emergent narrative or diverse narratives that arise from a community. 'Meaning' acts both as the legacy (output) of learning as well as a schema for the community's ongoing sense-making: perceiving, decision-making, and action all take place within a fluid complexity of ideas, identities, and interpretations, all of which individuals and organisations must learn to navigate" (Stodd et al., 2023). Students using GAI tools can use them to connect with each other, the instructor and the knowledge they are constructing, in learning that is active, social, generative, inquiry-based and constructivist by design.

There are many proven strategies to help build community: From group work to peer instruction, course design has an impact on the classroom experience, whether that class is in-person or online. Sharples's *Practical Pedagogy* (2019) suggests numerous examples of ways to build community, from creating a welcoming environment to establishing shared class norms to planning for collaborative projects that encourage teamwork. In digital environments, community is just as important, if not more so, but that community needs to be cultivated. How can we build a strong community in an AI-enabled learning environment? How does AI as presence impact this community? How can we design social learning using GAI presences in a way that augments rather than detracts from the learning experience? We can, for example, assign personas to GAI but we also need to remind students that AI is not a person (Veletsianos et al., 2024), because as we have seen in previous chapters the temptation to anthropomorphise AI is very natural and quite strong due to the conversational nature of GAI. So we can use the generative and social affordances of GAI but we must do so carefully and consciously, to ensure that these alien presences are helpful rather than hurtful.

5.7 Affective Computing

Not everything in education is about building cognitive skills, as any parent, counsellor or coach knows, which is why Bloom also created a taxonomy for the affective domain. Csikszentmihalyi's *Flow* (1991) taught us that being "in the zone" (i.e., a state of complete concentration or absorption) is conducive not just to learning but to happiness and productivity. This will not be particularly revelatory for anyone who has trained for a sport or plays music but achieving this in a classroom environment is altogether different. We know as educators that the task level has to be optimised but that the student also needs to be motivated to learn. How can AI assist with that motivation? Research has increased on the emotional and affective side of AI development from cognitive and educational psychologists (Gentile et al., 2023) but the application of research on emotions is extremely sensitive. AI-powered proctoring systems that monitor the user's eye movements have been rejected by many educational institutions as a breach of privacy. Similarly, pushback against the proposed use of biometric technologies for facial and emotional recognition (Barkane, 2022) in the EU AI Act called for stronger legal requirements for the use of such technologies, and when the Act passed in early 2024, the use of affective computing and systems that gauge student engagement or emotional responses during lectures based on facial recognition or voice analysis were forbidden.

Still, affective computing is an area of development for AI researchers and one of the early success stories from the 2023 GAI boom was Inflection AI's Pi chatbot. Billed as "your personal AI," Pi was an empathetic counterpart to other, less emotionally aware bots, which rather than asking how it could help asked "how's your day going?" and invited users to share how they were feeling. Inflection's early success was reflected in the huge investment it gained in early 2024, so it shocked the AI world when CEO Mustafa Suleyman and much of its staff defected to Microsoft in the strange case of the big tech non-acquisition of Inflection's talent. As discussed in Chap. 2, that move in particular highlighted the consolidation underway across the industry in 2024, as big tech and AI start-up partnerships were concentrated in three familiar names: Microsoft, Amazon, Google. But affective computing did not die with the purge in Inflection AI. Just weeks later, a new AI start-up named Hume AI, billed as "the first AI with emotional intelligence" raised $50 million in Series B funding. Hume uses an intelligent voice interface trained on an its eLLM (empathetic LLM), which measures vocal modulations, guiding language and speech generation, capturing nuance in expressions in audio, video and images. Founded in 2021 by Google researcher Allan Cowen, Hume aims to build an emotionally intelligent conversational AI that can interpret emotions based on how people are speaking and generate an appropriate response" (Shrivastava, 2024).

5.8 Social AI

Conversational AI is already integrated across many of our tools and platforms and the immense popularity of platforms like Character.ai and AI companions shows the potential for social and emotional AI. Voice-activated translation is already widespread and GPT's voice is now in Figure's 01 humanoid robot. Open AI's Voice Engine, a tool in development since late 2022, powers the Read Aloud feature in ChatGPT (David, 2024a), which can read text prompts in the language of the speaker or in a number of others. Voice Engine requires only a 15-s sample to clone a human voice (David, 2024b) and was not released to the wider public because of concerns over potential uses by bad actors during the 2024 election year. The risk posed by AI voices, combined with text-to-video technology for deepfakes, is clear and recognised. The potential benefits for education of synthetic media are also real. Being able to generate voices in any language for videos and to converse with others in any language, simultaneously, using voice-activated AI tools, means that linguistic barriers will effectively cease to exist. Some have predicted this will spell the end of foreign-language education (Matsakis, 2024) but it is more likely that practice will simply adapt and change.

One thing is certain: Research combining affective computing and the rapid growth in conversational AI is moving GAI into the affective realm via our shared social spaces. Mishra argues that it is more useful to think about GAI tools in terms of a presence in the learning community than as a set of tools standing outside of it (Mishra et al, 2023). Indeed, "GenAI will require educators to develop new pedagogies and recognise that there will be other social agents in the learning space, a space that has primarily inhabited by humans" (Gentile et al., 2023). Having AI in the classroom means having multiple experts available for every single student, who is ready and able to give them personalised attention that one human simply cannot. "Their true potential manifests when utilized as an expert collaborator, one who often gets things wrong but who can help with a range of complex tasks such as comparing concepts, constructing counter arguments, generating analogies, analysing data, or evaluating symbolic logic." (Mishra, 2023, p. 242) We are now looking at a future for education that includes multiple human plus AIs in the classroom.

This is likely to accelerate the shift in the role of the educator from primary source of authority to facilitator, as GAI social agents represent a disruption to our conception of the agency of the learner and the role of the teacher. GAI social agents will perform better than humans in many aspects, potentially challenging the traditional role of the educator as expert. They will also be increasingly autonomous presences, as "technology, which until now has always played a material role, is becoming an agent in its own right." (Gentile et al., 2023). Sharing the learning space with autonomous agents means that that "rather than identifying AI as an antagonist, educators must learn to coexist with it, moving from a binary (student-learner) to a ternary (student-learner-machine) relationship in which interactions are mediated, modified, and sometimes initiated by technology" (Gentile et al., 2023). The

5.8 Social AI

role of educator as mediator in this complex environment will become increasingly important but the new shape will not suit everyone.

In 2024, Ferris State University announced its plans to admit two AI students to a course in its AI programme. The AI students were trained using data from student surveys and their presence was intended to discover more about the student experience but having two AI students "sit in" on a campus class obviously brings up many issues to do with surveillance, monitoring and privacy, as they will be recording conversations that take place between real students and the instructor in their classes. What effect does having an AI student in the class have on student behaviour—can/will they still speak freely? How—if at all—is the data used for instructor evaluations? The issues here clearly go beyond the standard data privacy issues to those around performance, freedom of speech and potentially to academic and intellectual freedom—all key on any campus.

Social and autonomous AI agents will change the nature of communication in digital spaces. "In contrast to traditional social media that offers tools to support person-to-person connection, GenAI encourages social interaction through the tool itself. This ability to engage as if it were human is a unique development in the history of technology" (Mishra, 2023, p. 241). Early research investigating the dynamics between AI and learners indicated that "participants imagine AI-learner relationships with AI on a continuum, viewing AI as an object on the one end and as a subject on the other. In the first view, participants see AI as a tool for learning or a tool in the service of learning. In contrast, participants with the second view orient to AI as a subject, i.e., as one who has agency and possibly some kind of internal subjectivity," with many participants merging the two (Veletsianos et al., 2024). The potential for harm and the diversity of views and learner needs highlight the need for guardrails to protect students from being influenced by harmful attitudes in the AI's training data that might surface during interaction. Veletsianos et al. caution that educators and designers will "need to account for the diverse spectrum of ways people will or could relate to AI" and warn that there are already concerns about the way that people have interacted with AI. This calls for intentional design, to ensure the shared learning space is a positive, equitable, accessible and inclusive space for interaction between human students and instructors, along with GAI social agents.

What does this mean for learning? On the one hand, we have experts in everything available. But it is the AI's ability to initialise interaction, to configure itself as a communicator on par with the human that also poses the challenge and having GAI experts and peers in the learning community has important implications for the dynamic between educators and students. GAI's unique affordances therefore require a new approach to pedagogy and practice that can frame how to communicate and construct meaning through conversation with digital peers. Designing the space where learners interact with GAI also needs to be approached with great care to ensure that GAI's social affordances are used to create learning experiences that are AI-powered and human-centred.

Sharples has argued that "as GenAI becomes embedded into office tools and social media, it will bring new opportunities and challenges for social interaction between humans and AI." (Sharples, 2023, p. 160) Drawing on AI in education pioneer Pask's work, Sharples argues that "a systems view of cognition distributed among humans and AI agents open possibilities of new internet tools to enhance conversation, and of the Web for social learning among humans and AI." While we do not have such a system in place yet, the notion of persistent conversations over time (i.e., beyond the single prompt + response) is possible thanks to the increased memory of GAI models and the personalisation that brings. Sharples argues that "generative AI has the potential to contribute to this social learning process of setting shared goals, performing tasks together, exploring possibilities, and conversing to reach agreements" (Sharples, 2023). With this, we can see how the social affordances of GAI can be used to create a shared educational experience that sees humans and AIs collaborating in learning.

How do we design social learning that includes both humans and AIs? What might sorts of presences might alien intelligences bring to the learning space? And how do we create community in a space that is now shared by multiple intelligences? Just as the Conversational Framework helped frame the interaction with GAI to design active and generative learning designed using pedagogically sound principles, the Community of Inquiry framework can help us to design a learning community that includes both human and AI presences, and maybe even enable us to use these alien intelligences to augment our own (Shadbolt, 2022). By designing the learning environment to tap into GAI's social affordances, educators can use these presences constructively and creatively as part of the learning experience.

5.9 Intelligent Communities

In online learning, creating community among distance learners has been underway for over two decades and the frameworks that have been used successfully to build community in digital environments lend themselves well to the use of GAI. Two are particularly useful for educators exploring designing learning communities that include GAI. The first, Online Collaborative Learning, is a model of learning that encourages students working together to construct knowledge that was developed into online collaborative theory (Harasim, 2017).

Echoing Generativism's focus on sense-making, Harasim describes OCL as providing "a model of learning in which students are encouraged and supported to work together to create knowledge: to invent, to explore ways to innovate, and, by so doing, to seek the conceptual knowledge needed to solve problems rather than recite what they think is the right answer."

Harasim alternately describes OCL as "a form of constructivist teaching that takes the form of instructor-led group learning online [where] students are encouraged to collaboratively solve problems through discourse instead of memorizing correct answers. The teacher plays a crucial role as a facilitator as well as a member of the knowledge community under study" (Harasim, n.d.). The educator-as-facilitator plays a key role in digital communities, creating the context for learning and functioning as the link between the knowledge community and the learner. "The teacher plays a key role not as a fellow-learner, but as the link to the knowledge community, or state of the art in the discipline" (Harasim, 2017). This characterisation of the educator as the critical link between the knowledge community recalls Connectivism's description of nodes in the digital network and underlines the importance of the educator as the mediator of what is no longer simply content *knowledge* but now content *intelligence*. While GAI has access to the sum of the world's knowledge on a particular topic, the educator is the disciplinary expert in this constructivist, connectivist, generative and social learning community, who can help students interpret output and discern between hallucinations and useful information, and hone their critical and analytical skills.

5.10 Collaborative Learning

The second framework is the Community of Inquiry (CoI) (Garrison et al., 2000; Garrison, 2007, 2015, 2017, 2020; Garrison & Akyol, 2013; Garrison & Vaughan, 2007) which has been used to foster students' critical thinking skills through inquiry-based learning (Kaczkó & Ostendorf, 2023), for blended learning (Vaughan et al., 2013), and in empirical studies to support academic staff and faculty development (Vaughan & Garrison, 2006). Recalling generative learning theory, Garrison describes the CoI as a framework for the design of online education that helps students learn through active participation and shared meaning-making (Garrison, 2020). The CoI represents "a process of creating a deep and meaningful (collaborative-constructivist) learning experience through the development of three interdependent elements—social, cognitive and teaching presence."

Social presence is "the ability of participants to identify with the community (e.g., course of study), communicate purposefully in a trusting environment, and develop inter-personal relationships by way of projecting their individual personalities. Teaching Presence is "the design, facilitation, and direction of cognitive and social processes for the purpose of realising personally meaningful and educationally worthwhile learning outcomes" and Cognitive Presence is "the extent to which learners can construct and confirm meaning through sustained reflection and discourse (CoI; Garrison et al., 2000).

The question of how to bring these ideas to life, to create the conditions for learning and to move from the realm of ideas to implementation is where learning design comes in. Garrison has asked, "what effect will AI have on online communities of inquiry?" and points out that " the challenge is using this resource to enhance critical thinking and collaborative learning" (Garrison, 2023). The generative and social affordances of GAI make the CoI particularly well suited for use in social inquiry-based learning that includes GAI as a presence in the community. The framework's three forms of presence (teaching presence, cognitive presence and social presence) offers a starting point from which to extend the learning community to include AI tutors, experts and classmates, and to design learning that uses conversation and interaction with GAI as part of the learning process.

GAI tutors, experts, buddies, mentors, coaches (or an array of other types of actors) brings a new dimension to the CoI's collaborative and constructivist approach. Generativism invites us to reimagine each of these three those forms of presence, with GAI agents recast as actors that interact with learners in the Community: Social Presence becomes "Collaborator AI", where students engage and work with other actors, as well as the instructor and peers. Cognitive Presence becomes "Analytical AI", where agents provide perspectives on a given topic and function as a companion, opponent and/or coach. Teaching Presence becomes "Facilitator AI", where AI tutors function as guides on the side that accompany and support the student throughout the course. The Community of Inquiry Framework therefore helps us place these alien presences within the learning space and to use their affordances in personalised and peer learning that is social, collaborative, inquiry-based and human-centred (Fig. 5.1).

The roles that GAI can take on are really only limited by our own imaginations. A GAI social agent can be a guide, peer, expert or any other sort of collaborator in the learning community, or it can simply play the role of a guide-on-the-side that accompanies and supports the student as they progress through the course. Sharples has suggested several roles for GAI in cooperative and social learning, including a possibility engine, to generate alternative ways of expressing an idea; a Socratic opponent, acting as a respondent to develop an argument; a collaboration coach, to help groups research and solve problems together; a co-designer, to assist through the design process; an exploratorium, which provides tools to play with, explore and interpret data; and a storyteller, to create stories that include diverse views, abilities and experiences (Sharples, 2023, Table 1, p. 162). These are just some of the many roles that GAI can play in collaborative inquiry-based learning. Mollick has suggested many ways to use GAI as a creative partner in ideation for entrepreneurial activities and as a productivity-boosting assistant (Mollick 2023/24 blog; Mollick, 2024) in workplace environments. Combining the CoI framework with GAI actors and using new categories like Collaborative, Analytical and Facilitator AI allows us

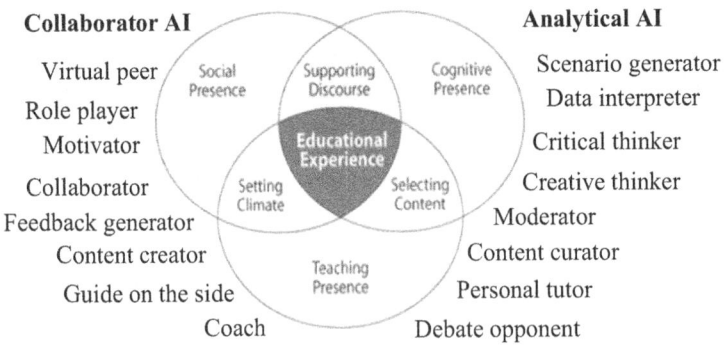

Fig. 5.1 Community of inquiry + AI

to situate GAI within the educational experience and use it to design and deliver learning activities in collaboration with AI.

But a note of caution is required, as GAI is an emerging technology that must be used with great care in educational environments. We know that AI model training is biased toward a certain demographic (white, male, North American) and even with the development of sovereign AI it will take years to change this. There are several different types of LLMs and ways to train emerging models. Anthropic, for example, uses what it calls Constitutional AI, which is AI that has been trained using documents including the UN Declaration of Human Rights (Sharples, 2023). This means that Anthropic's Claude behaves very differently from Elon Musk's Grok, which Musk created to be as free and wild as possible. While Grok would be an excellent choice for practicing adversarial thinking, it would not be suitable for a healthy and productive discussion on neurodiversity or inclusion. This is why educators need to be AI literate, so they know the difference between models like Claude and Grok and understand why one might be a better bet for a certain assignment or activity than another. They need to be informed enough to develop strategies "to protect learners and foster more relational (and therefore more realistic and complex) ways of interacting with AI" (Veletsianos et al., 2024).

This means working directly with the technology, to understand firsthand how it behaves and how to use it responsibly. There is much more to be done yet to understand the relationships between humans and AI and Veletsianos' call for diversity of representation and recognition of varied experiences must form the basis of future work. This is also why the legal principles expressed in the EU's AI Act are so important. While some object to such regulation as stifling innovation, for GAI to be used in educational settings, it must be reliable, trustworthy, and humane. "Designing new social AI systems for education requires more than fine tuning existing language models for educational purposes. It requires building GenAI to follow fundamental human rights, respect the expertise of teachers and care for the diversity and development of students" (Sharples, 2023). This system does not yet exist. For now, we have an emergent technology, laden with problems. Until that exists, it will be educators, those working with this technology on the front lines with students, that play an active part in shaping its development. Indeed, they must, as only by doing so will AI become representative of what it means to be fully human.

References

Armstrong, A. (2023, March 29). [blog] We're trialling an online AI Teaching Assistant. Online Education at the University of London. https://onlinelearning.london.ac.uk/2023/03/29/ai-teaching-assistant-pilot/

Barkane, I. (2022). Questioning the EU proposal for an artificial intelligence act: The need for prohibitions and a stricter approach to biometric surveillance. *Information Polity, 27*(2022), 147–162.

Bates, A. W. (2019). *Teaching in a digital age—Third edition*. Tony Bates Associates Ltd. https://pressbooks.bccampus.ca/teachinginadigitalagev2/

Bloom, B. S. (1984). The 2 sigma problem: The search for methods of group instruction as effective as one-to-one tutoring. *Educational Researcher, 13*, 4–16.

Chassignol, M., Khoroshavin, A., Klimova, A., & Bilyatdinova, A. (2018). Artificial Intelligence trends in education: A narrative overview. *Procedia Computer Science, 136*, 16–24.

CoI Framework. Athabasca University. https://coi.athabascau.ca/coi-model/

Csikszentmihalyi, M. (1991). *Flow: The psychology of optimal experience: Steps toward enhancing the quality of life*. Harper Collins Publishers.

David, E. (2024a, March 4). ChatGPT can read its answers out loud. *The Verge*. https://www.theverge.com/2024/3/4/24090500/chatgpt-openai-voice-ios-android

David, E. (2024b, March 29). OpenAI's voice cloning AI model only needs a 15-second sample to work. *The Verge*. https://www.theverge.com/2024/3/29/24115701/openai-voice-generation-ai-model

European Commission. (2024, March 6). Shaping Europe's digital future: AI act [blog]. https://digital-strategy.ec.europa.eu/en/policies/regulatory-framework-ai

Garrison, D. R. (2007). Online community of inquiry review: Social, cognitive, and teaching presence issues. *Journal of Asynchronous Learning Networks, 11*(1), 61–72.

Garrison, D. R. (2015). *Thinking collaboratively: Learning in a community of inquiry*. Routledge.

Garrison, D. R. (2017). *E-learning in the 21st century: A community of inquiry framework for research and practice*. Taylor & Francis.

Garrison, D. R., & Akyol, Z. (2013). The community of inquiry theoretical framework. *Handbook of Distance Education, 3*, 104–120.

Garrison, D. R., Anderson, T., & Archer, W. (2000). Critical inquiry in a text-based environment: Computer conferencing in higher education. *The Internet and Higher Education, 2*, 87–105. https://doi.org/10.1016/S1096-7516(00)00016-6

Garrison, R. (2020). Reflective teaching in a digital age. *Buzzsprout* [podcast interview]. https://reflectiveteaching.buzzsprout.com/1384834/5950516

Garrison, R. (2023, May 19). Online learning and AI. *Community of inquiry* [blog]. https://www.thecommunityofinquiry.org/editorial41

Garrison, R., & Vaughan, N. D. (2007). *Blended learning in higher education: Framework, principles and guidelines*. Wiley Press.

Gentile, M., Città, G., Perna, S., & Allegra, M. (2023). Do we still need teachers? Navigating the paradigm shift of the teacher's role in the AI era. *Frontiers in Education, 8*, 1161777. https://doi.org/10.3389/feduc.2023.1161777

Goel, A., Dede, C., Garn, M., & Ou, C. (2024, January). AI-ALOE: AI for reskilling, upskilling, and workforce development. *AI Magazine*. https://doi.org/10.1002/aaai.12157

Guo, L., et al. (2021). Evolution and trends in intelligent tutoring systems research: A multidisciplinary and scientometric view. *Asia Pacific Education Review, 2021*(22), 441–461. https://doi.org/10.1007/s12564-021-09697-7

Harasim, L. (2017). *Learning theory and online technologies* (2nd ed.). Taylor and Francis.

Harasim, L. (n.d.). Online collaborative learning theory. Retrieved from https://www.lindaharasim.com/online-collaborative-learning/.

Kaczkó, É., & Ostendorf, A. (2023). Critical thinking in the community of inquiry framework: An analysis of the theoretical model and cognitive presence coding schemes. *Computers & Education, 193*. https://doi.org/10.1016/j.compedu.2022.104662

Luckin, R., Holmes, W., Griffiths, M., & Forcier, L. B. (2016). *Intelligence unleashed: An argument for AI in education*. Pearson.

Matsakis, L. (2024, March 26). The end of foreign-language education. *The Atlantic*. https://www.theatlantic.com/technology/archive/2024/03/generative-ai-translation-education/677883/

Mishra, P., Warr, M., & Islam, R. (2023). TPACK in the age of ChatGPT and generative AI. *Journal of Digital Learning in Teacher Education, 39*(4), 235–251. https://doi.org/10.1080/21532974.2023.2247480

Mollick, E. (2023–24) *One useful thing*. Substack [blog]. https://www.oneusefulthing.org/

Mollick, E. (2024). *Co-intelligence: Living and working with AI*. Penguin.

References

Mollick, E. R., & Mollick, L. (2024). Instructors as innovators: A future-focused approach to new AI learning opportunities, with prompts. https://doi.org/10.2139/ssrn.4802463

OpenAI Index. (n.d.). Khan academy explores the potential for GPT-4 in a limited pilot program. https://openai.com/index/khan-academy

Rogerson, T. (2024, March 29). LinkedIn post. https://www.linkedin.com/feed/update/urn:li:activity:7179529602594144256/

Selwyn, N. (2019). *Should robots replace teachers? AI and the future of education.* Polity Press.

Shadbolt, N. (2022). "From so simple a beginning": Species of artificial intelligence. *Daedalus, 151*(2), 28–42. https://doi.org/10.1162/daed_a_01898.

Sharples, M. (2019). *Practical pedagogy: 40 new ways to teach and learn.* Taylor & Francis Group.

Sharples, M. (2023). Towards social generative AI for education: theory, practices and ethics. *Learning: Research and Practice, 9*, 2, 159–167. https://doi.org/10.1080/23735082.2023.2261131

Shrivastava, R. (2024, March 27). Feeling sad, excited or bored? This start-up claims its AI can (mostly) tell. *Forbes.* https://www.forbes.com/sites/rashishrivastava/2024/03/27/feeling-sad-excited-or-bored-this-startup-claims-its-ai-can-mostly-tell/

Sleeman, D. H., & Brown, J. S. (1982). *Intelligent tutoring systems: An overview.* New York: Academic Press.

St-Hilare, F., et al. (2023, March 3). A new era: Intelligent tutoring systems will transform online learning for millions. https://arxiv.org/abs/2203.03724. https://doi.org/10.48550/arXiv.2203.03724

Stodd, J., Schatz, S., & Stead, G. (2023). *Engines of engagement: A curious book about generative AI.* Sea Salt Publishing.

Veletsianos, G., Houlden, S., & Johnson, N. (2024). Is artificial intelligence in education an object or a subject? Evidence from a story completion exercise on learner-AI interactions. *TechTrends.* https://doi.org/10.1007/s11528-024-00942-5

Vaughan, N. D., Cleveland-Innes, M., & Garrison, D. R. (2013). *Teaching in blended learning environments: Creating and sustaining communities of inquiry.* Athabasca University Press.

Vaughan, N. D., & Garrison, R. (2006). How blended learning can support a faculty development community of inquiry. *Online Learning, 10*(4).

West, M. (2023). *An ed-tech tragedy? Educational technologies and school closures in the time of COVID-19.* UNESCO. https://unesdoc.unesco.org/ark:/48223/pf0000386701

Chapter 6
Assessing Learning

Abstract This chapter looks at the implications of generative AI for assessment, proposing a shift from assessing of learning as output to a focus on the process by which knowledge is constructed. It considers the impact of GAI on accreditation standards and curricula, and considers the implications for assessment strategies.

Keywords Assessing learning · Post-plagiarism · AI skills and competencies · Future/transversal skills · Accreditation · Curriculum planning · Assessment as learning · Competency-based assessment · Human + AI assessment

6.1 Introduction

The wave of disruption unleashed by the release of ChatGPT-3.5 on 30 November 2022 was followed by a huge wave of hype driven by technology fans and a corresponding wave of panic from higher education. The first two months of 2023 saw a relentless tide of increasingly alarmist headlines proclaiming that disaster was nigh: "The college essay is dead!" "No one is prepared!" "Should professors worry?" "Will it replace humans?" and "Could AI write your next paper?" Academics were quick to test ChatGPT-3.5 for themselves to find out just how dire the situation was, confirming that their essays were indeed an easy target. The first academic paper appeared, warning educators of the grave threat that ChatGPT posed to academic integrity (Susnjak, 2022). By mid-December, the key players entered the conversation about plagiarism detection, and the CEO of Turnitin, the popular anti-plagiarism tool integrated into campus LMS, promised an AI detector was coming soon. But detection technology was not sufficiently reliable to be used to identify cheating in student work with any degree of certainty and knee-jerk reactions abounded, as policy was decided on the fly, with little to no information. Schools in the USA banned the use of ChatGPT and Australian universities reverted to pen-and-paper exams. The latter changed tack just over week later, deciding with the benefit of some deliberation that ChatGPT could be used but only if cited as a source. On 4 January 2023, Princeton student Edward Tian released his GPTZero, which claimed to detect

AI-generated text based on its levels of "perplexity" and "burstiness"—indicators of a piece of text's humanness by virtue of its natural variation and unpredictability. The release sparked such interest that the site was down for most of the next few weeks. Tian and his team quickly followed up with GPTZero for Educators and in February announced a plug-in for Blackboard, Canvas, and Moodle. Open AI announced it would also be adding watermarks to GPT-generated text and Turnitin finally added its eagerly awaited GPT detector. Education administrators exhaled.

But when GPT-4 was released in March 2023, it showed a dramatic improvement in capabilities. No longer generating mid-range essays, GPT-4 was now acing a wide variety of standardised tests used the world over to select candidates for advanced degrees. This was the existential moment for academia, when it became clear that GAI was capable of much more than those early tests had revealed and much better than the formulaic essays with fabricated citations had suggested. GPT-4's capabilities continued to grow by leaps and bounds throughout 2023, starting with the addition of Code Interpreter (later named Advanced Data Analysis) and access to a plethora of other tools via OpenAI's Plug-in Store. By summer 2023, the core set of GAI chatbots could draft, write, and edit text; write and correct code; and generate images (Mollick, 2022).

Meanwhile, detectors proved unreliable, even discriminatory, producing high rates of false positives and tending to target content written by those whose first language is not English. As the evidence piled up it led to some high-profile withdrawals: In mid-2023 Open AI removed its detector from the market and Vanderbilt University disabled its Turnitin AI detector, both citing its concerns over inaccuracy. By July 2023, the advice was clear: "As tempting as it is to rely on AI tools to detect AI-generated writing, evidence so far has shown that they are not reliable. Due to false positives, AI writing detectors such as GPTZero, ZeroGPT and OpenAI's Text Classifier cannot be trusted to detect text composed by Large Language models (LLMs) like ChatGPT" (Edwards, 2023). Recommendations to embrace GAI in assessment (Ardito, 2023) were supported by subsequent research, which confirmed that "the accuracy limitations and the potential for false accusations demonstrate that these tools cannot currently be recommended for determining whether violations of academic integrity have occurred" (Perkins et al., 2024). Meanwhile, in a tragi-comedic display of the force of Schumpeter's creative destruction, numerous AI tools for students emerged, offering to rewrite assignments until they were detector-proof and provide answers to multiple-choice tests, rendering them useless other than for formative self-assessment.

As time went on, the line between using AI to cheat and as a legitimate assistive technology became blurred. A student in the USA was sanctioned for using Grammarly, the ubiquitous writing tool in every students' digital toolkit, which like almost all of the tools in the former digital ecosystem, is now AI-powered. Turnitin's AI detection system flagged her criminal justice paper as robot-generated and the student received a zero, which lowered her grade point average to the extent that she also missed out on a scholarship. She insisted the work was her own and posted a warning video for others on TikTok, which racked up over 5.5 million views by

April 2024 (Young, 2024). This episode highlighted the urgent need for AI literacy for students, instructors and administrators alike.

6.2 The Canary in the Coalmine

This reliance on technology to solve a bigger problem in education is not new. Over decades, higher education has become increasingly dependent on anti-plagiarism systems to decide whether or not a student has cheated on their submission. The automating of anti-plagiarism has meant that students accused of cheating are presumed guilty and have to defend themselves—the exact opposite of how it works in a justice system. The use of AI detectors has resulted in numerous cases of students being falsely accused of cheating and the corrosive effect of this cycle of blame and fear, augmented by the use of detection technology, has resulted in students reporting being afraid to use GAI in their work—not because of a fear of the technology itself but because of a fear of being accused of cheating. The education sector is already struggling to cope with the increased levels of mental health issues among students, so casting students as would-be cheaters from the outset, thereby elevating those levels of anxiety further, is a difficult decision to fathom. Indeed, it is entirely at odds with the narrative at many institutions around the need to foster a sense of belonging and pedagogies of care. Instead of care, students suffered from a lack of guidance and leadership that was regressive and, in some cases, personally damaging.

This reaction also hit institutions where it hurt, resulting in increased administrative work for those already struggling to facilitate the multitude of requests for accommodation. Accusing students of cheating is an expensive business. In early 2024, it was reported that at several UK universities, the costs associated with anti-plagiarism measures in the UK had skyrocketed (Khaleel et al., 2024). The dramatic increase in spending came at a time when higher education was already under tremendous financial strain. Policing students is not only a poor approach in terms of trust, it is also financially unsustainable, and the conversation about assessment is not really about assessment at all—GAI has only amplified pre-existing problems of the over-reliance on platform solutions in place of human relationships in a system that is rapidly losing student trust and choking it its own bureaucratic red tape. Assessment is the canary in the coalmine that institutional leaders ignore at their peril.

6.3 Stop-Gap Measures

Change is difficult and education is particularly resistant to it. While the writing on the wall was clearly visible for traditional assessment, rather than investing in the rethinking and redesign that is required, institutional leaders continue to look for stop-gap solutions to prolong the longevity of traditional assesssment approaches. Some of the motivation is legitimate—integrity of assessment is tied to professional acccredition and institutional reputation—but much of the reluctance to change is a product of the model itself.

6.3.1 The Return to Pen-And-Paper

In December 2022, a paper on the so-called end of integrity in online exams claimed that the only way to stay ahead of generative AI was to exploit its weaknesses (Susnjak, 2022). The suggestions therein to preserve the integrity of online assessments therefore consisted of recommendations to use multi-modal input or revert to pen-and-paper tests. GAI became multi-modal in early 2023, so the first recommendation was no longer viable, but the interest in preserving final written exams has persisted as a means to maintain academic integrity. In February 2024, Glasgow University announced a return to in-person Life Science exams for students in years three and four, citing a need to ensure reliability in exam results to would-be employers—a move that sparked predictable anger from students (Scott & Bonar, 2024). Since the Covid-19 pandemic, many exams had been delivered online, so students were not accustomed to handwriting final exam papers. Aside from that, the practice of handwriting itself has declined in the digital age, so reverting to pen-and-paper exams for a generation of students more used to texting than writing was slightly perverse.

But this episode highlighted the more important issue for many institutions, which was the need to ensure that the grades and degrees they issue are reliable—particularly for those linked to medical practice, where quality standards and professional accreditation are closely intertwined. As the University spokesperson put it, "We are taking this step so that we can assure…the quality bodies that accredit degrees, as well as future employers—that the Life Sciences exams are reliable" (Scott & Bonar, 2024). The issue is not so much cheating, it is that universities and colleges need to be able to guarantee the reliability of their degrees. There is no getting around the fact that the "product" of higher education institutions is competent graduates, and should the standards of those graduates fall or be called into question, it has a direct bearing on the institution that trained them. The need to guarantee academic integrity is as much about institutional reputation as it is about student learning.

6.3.2 AI-Assisted Grading

While pen-and-paper exams are not scalable, ironically, AI might enable the longevity of this distinctly AI-unfriendly approach to assessment. Digital assessment platforms already offer the option to upload handwritten texts, which AI tools can grade. Several platforms exist that offer instructors the opportunity to automate their grading and provide feedback using AI assistants. Some of these platforms existed before GAI hit the mainstream in late 2022 and have since added GAI to their offering, just as the

6.3 Stop-Gap Measures

many formerly digital tools in ecosystem have become AI-powered. Others are new start-ups, products of the GAI era. Using AI-assisted grading offers an easy route from the current platform model, and as such, offer another stop-gap measure that allows instructors and institutions to extend the life of assessment types that many would argue have had their day. While such platforms can certainly help by making the process of marking assessments more efficient, AI-assisted grading platforms alone do not address the bigger issue of needing to replace vulnerable assessment types with more sustainable models. As with resource generators, there is also a danger that in becoming dependent on such platforms to solve these bigger problems, we risk ignoring the real issue, which is the need to redesign assessment for the AI age.

6.3.3 From 0 to 5

Introducing GAI gradually into assessment has been a popular approach in writing courses. The AI Assessment Scale (Perkins et al., 2023) progresses gradually from assessments with "no AI," where any use of AI is strictly forbidden, to "full AI," where AI is used as a co-pilot and the work is acknowledged to be the product of human-plus-AI collaboration. First published in 2023, it was intended as "a practical, flexible approach that can be implemented quickly" that gave educators a way into dealing with the challenges of integrated GAI into text-heavy assessments. The assessment scale is aimed primarily at instructors using writing tasks at the K-12 levels and the authors take a tools-focused approach that reflects their hesitation around the uses of GAI given the state of policy and on the ethics of using GAI with younger students. As such, it is a useful mechanism to open discussion about the ethical uses of GAI and to introduce some of the basic concepts around AI literacy.

The AI scale is another way to frame SAMR's four levels of substitution, augmentation, modification and transformation, and it is clear that over the longer-term, GAI will require more than mere substitution or modification, but full transformation. The key issue is that, as per the discussion on TPACK, that with the shift from domain knowledge to domain *intelligence*, there is a bigger shift at play, and that shift is common to *all* disciplinary practices. So, just as the narrative about cheating is really about institutional reputation and accreditation standards, so the issue about writing with GAI is the fact that the *practice* of writing has changed. Collaboration with GAI is changing disciplinary practices, so as we move from TPACK to TPAIK, the vast majority of assessments will require full transformation because the skills and competencies they measure will change.

Eaton argues that we have already entered the post-plagiarism era, "in which advanced technologies such as artificial intelligence and neurotechnology, including brain-computer interfaces (BCIs), become a normal part of life, including how we teach, learn, communicate, and interact on a daily basis" (Eaton, 2023a, 2023b). Standard definitions of academic malpractice therefore no longer apply and hybrid human-AI writing is just one manifestation of this new reality. This is not an issue restricted to students—academic publications have been some of the most high-profile of those impacted by the influx of AI-assisted research and writing. Scientific papers appear to be particularly vulnerable, with one estimate from a researcher at University College London putting the number of academic papers published in 2023 written in full or in part by AI at 60,000 (Gray, 2024) and another from Stanford at between 6 and 17%, depending on the topic (Liang et al., 2024). The question now is how to deal with it, as students, researchers and educators of all stripes have incorporated GAI into their workflow (Conde et al., 2024).

Stop-gap measures are legitimate approaches to buy the sector some time to introduce GAI to students and staff and to deal with the basics of AI literacy. But they are not a solution to the bigger and longer-term challenge, which is that GAI "forces us to acknowledge that many of our assessments do not truly measure student understanding and knowledge" (Mishra et al., 2023) and certainly not the new knowledge, skills and competencies that the AI age requires.

6.4 Mapping the Future

Educational institutions confer degrees that are based on the assessment of learning defined by certain knowledge, skills and competencies. For professional degrees, those competencies are mapped to their own frameworks for professional standards. Learning is now being measured with assessments that can no longer be trusted and mapped to learning outcomes that will soon be out of date. While this might not be life or death in Music or History, in an area like Nursing or Engineering it is, and industry standards must change to reflect the new AI world we live in. In April 2024, an opinion piece published in *Inside Higher Ed* (Justus & Janos, 2024) called for accreditation bodies to weigh in and assist with the redesign of assessment for the age of GAI. This is urgent work for all professional associations—to update the professional competencies specific to their field.

Assessment is directly tied to the professional accreditation bodies that regulate those industries. Assessment and accreditation are intertwined, so when professional standards of industry bodies change, assessment of skills and competencies must also change. It follows then that course-and programme-level outcomes must also address the updated skills and competencies that students need to perform the tasks required of them in those roles. Assessment must change—not because of worries about cheating but because it is critical that educational institutions prepare students to meet the professional standards of this new world.

From the creative industries to the hard sciences, every discipline is being transformed by the interaction with GAI. Whether or not assessment is tied to professional accreditation, ignoring this reality is the real existential risk to education. Educational institutions must revisit the knowledge, skills and competencies that their assessments currently measure, and as those standards change, the outcomes by which we assess our students must also change. Curriculum mapping projects must take place across every educational institution, to update and redefine the knowledge, skills and competencies in each discipline for the AI age.

6.5 Competencies for the AI Age

When GAI first hit the mainstream, much of the focus was correctly placed on building basic AI literacy. The expectation was that once educators, with the guidance and support of their institutions, had built that basic AI literacy, they would progress in a scaffolded process from learning *about* AI to learning *for* and *with* AI (European Commission, 2023). But building AI literacy is just the start. AI is redefining the skills and competencies that are needed to thrive in this world. Not only do we need to nurture so-called human or future skills or competencies, we also need to update the skills and competencies in hard disciplinary areas, where AI is changing practice. Assessments for the AI age will need to measure a combination of AI skills, human/future skills, and disciplinary skills and competencies.

6.5.1 AI Skills and Competencies

AI competencies are the basic skills required to work with AI. They include understanding how the technology works and the main issues and risks to be aware of when interacting with AI models. This is a vast area that extends from understanding the general landscape of development, including regulation, issues around ethics and AI development, and how to exercising critical judgment with that knowledge, to being aware of all of the issues to do with how the models are trained, issues around bias in the training data, risk and safety issues, including hallucinations. AI literacy teaches us to view such developments from a critical and informed standpoint. Examples like Google Gemini's early 2024 over-correction to include diversity in its image generation indicated the power of big tech to literally change our representation of real historical events (Gilbert, 2024). There are similar examples for every discipline and topic, and instructors need to be AI literate in order to bring such discussions to their classes. Luckily, there is now a wealth of resources, from competency frameworks (Lee, 2023) to courses available for beginners, so no individual educator need take this task on alone.

6.5.2 Future Human Skills

In 2016, the World Economic Forum identified 21st Century skills (Soffel, 2016) as critically important for the era of the Fourth Industrial Revolution (Skilton &

Hovsepian, 2018), where critical thinking, creativity, collaboration, resilience, leadership (to name a few) are needed to complement and offset the high-tech skills that define the digital workplace. Human or so-called future skills are sometimes referred to as transversal skills because they cut *across* disciplines and are needed in every industry. These are the skills we used to call "soft" skills, in contrast to the "hard" skills that are discipline-specific. They are the higher order skills that include being able to communicate well, to work in teams, to display leadership, to show initiative and to demonstrate resilience in the face of adversity. They are the skills related to our emotional rather than cognitive intelligence, our ability to be empathetic, and closely related to our self-development as human beings. They are the skills we have assured ourselves are uniquely human and cannot be replicated by AI. Human skills allow us to work with machines as equals, bringing different but complementary skills to the increasingly technical table. They are also the skills we need to prosper in the so-called VUCA world that is Volatile, Uncertain, Complex and Ambiguous. With "permacrisis" named as the word of the year in 2022 and with global crises multiplying year on year, we are told that these human skills will be more important than ever.

Thinking of competencies in terms of AI versus human can serve as a useful starting point for educators drafting a list of learning goals for a particular course or programme. Developing human skills allows us to develop our emotional intelligence and to use the affective capabilities that Bloom also identified to thrive in the AI world. Exercising our human skills is also a critical part of using AI literacy when interacting with GAI. It is also reassuring to think that certain attributes are quintessentially and irreplaceably "human" and therefore safe from the encroaching AI. But this binary of human and AI also has a looming expiry date: As AI exhibits increasingly impressive capabilities in areas many have historically categorised as human (i.e. creativity, collaboration and problem-solving) it will become increasingly difficult to draw the line between what humans do that AI cannot, and with the growth in affective computing and empathetic AI to classify competencies to do with emotional intelligence as uniquely human or AI. In future, this line will become increasingly blurred. But for now, these categories serve as a useful starting point for discussion and planning.

6.5.3 Domain Intelligence

Domain expertise is the area that educators typically begin with when creating a new course or syllabus, as those are most closely connected to their disciplinary expertise. It is still common practice for in-person educators to begin drafting a new course syllabus by listing content areas or topic headings that students are expected to understand by the end of a course or programme, which generally form the basis of their assessment. In digital design, the approach is the opposite, where best practice dictates that we begin with the end in mind, focusing on the skills and competencies that learners need to gain. Digital designers generally begin by defining the learning goals, then the assessment that measures how well the goals have been achieved. The learning activities are designed to teach the knowledge, skills and competencies that will be assessed, and the content or materials come at the very end. This is how backwards design works in practice.

GAI is now changing practice across all disciplines, which means that domain expertise will change with it. This means it will be increasingly difficult to separate domain-specific competencies from AI competencies. Indeed, they might become human + AI competencies. Historians are using GPT-Vision to read eighteenth century medical manuals (Breen, 2023) and projects like the Vesuvius scrolls promise to unlock history in a way we could not long ago only dream of (Weber, 2024). Research into student-researcher workflows shows the integration of ChatGPT for requesting, evaluating, and refining work (Pigg, 2024). It also confirms these shifts, highlighting the differing attitudes to using GAI among experts and those just learning how to conduct research. From History to Modern Languages to Film Studies to Computer Science to Medicine to Data Science—every academic discipline and practice will be changed by GAI.

This means that before beginning the task of redesigning a course or rewriting learning outcomes to integrate GAI, we need to ask some fundamental questions: How is GAI changing the subject we teach? What does that mean for our learning goals? What is now most important for our students to learn? What sorts of learning activities do we need to design to accomplish those goals? What can they learn independently or with AI that we no longer need to teach? How can we design learning using GAI as a collaborator or partner in learning? GAI is fundamentally changing the areas of knowledge that educators need to draw upon. These changes in our disciplines must be reflected in the learning goals that inform the assessments we design to measure learning.

6.6 Authentic Assessment

After the initial panic about ChatGPT and alongside the discussion about detectors, a more productive discussion began to take place about the need to use more authentic approaches (Elkhoury, 2020) to assessment than those traditionally used in many institutions of higher and continuing education. Such pedagogical ideas are not new—they are part of the movement toward more student-centred and constructivist learning approaches that view assessment is part of the learning process rather than separate from it—and increasingly relevant given the challenges to traditional assessment in light of AI. What is authentic assessment in the age of AI? What sort of assessments do we need in a world where AI can perform many of the tasks in the white-collar jobs in our knowledge economy? What sort of assessment is authentic in a world where jobs will require humans to work with AI? How do we prepare students for such a world? How do we assess for it? It does not make sense to design a course using AI as a collaborator and then revert to old-fashioned exams and essays, so we need to design assessments that are authentic in the AI world.

6.6.1 Interactive Orals (IO)

Oral assessments—a shorter version of the classic viva—are usually reserved for a defence of a major piece of work, such as a thesis or dissertation, but Interactive Orals (IOs) have been piloted as an alternative to exams at Griffith University in Australia and at Dublin City University in Ireland since the Covid-19 pandemic, as well as Singapore Institute of Technology (Logan & Sotiriadou, n.d.). Defined as an "efficient and effective form of authentic assessment that promotes skill development and employability, enhances overall student engagement and a personalised approach to learning and teaching, and preserves academic integrity," (DCU TEU) these experiments were originally conceived as temporary measures but have seen a resurgence of interest due to GAI. IOs allowed Griffith to assess student skill development and improve student employability prospects at the same time, by offering students the opportunity to engage in unscripted conversation. Findings indicated that IOs are an "efficient and effective form of authentic assessment that promotes skill development and employability, enhances overall student engagement and a personalised approach to learning and teaching, and preserves academic integrity" (Logan & Sotiriadou, n.d.). Dublin City University (DCU) has followed Griffith's lead in exploring IOs and is piloting their use as a robust model of authentic assessment design.

6.6.2 Scaling Authentic Assessment

The challenge with authentic assessments historically has been that they are difficult to scale but technology gives educators the tools to do so without adding to their workload. Best practice in digital design suggests using assessment rubrics for individual assignments and assessment. Doing so makes expectations clear to the student and helps cut down on pre-assessment anxiety by allowing students to prepare. Rubrics also assist the instructor in grading that work. Just as AI transcription tools are being used in the corporate world to record meetings and generate meeting notes and suggest actions, we can do the same for assessment. A student can join a virtual IO, which is recorded and transcribed by an AI transcription tool. Then, using the rubrics aligned to learning outcomes, AI generates draft feedback and grades based on the rubrics. Because GAI is conversational, it is not only useful for conversation-based learning activities but also conversation-based assessments. In the case of IOs, the assessment is designed around a conversation, prompting from the assessor, self-assessment by the student and feedback on performance—all based on a clear assessment rubric. These steps and this structure also lend themselves perfectly to the use of AI to make the delivery and marking more efficient. GAI can be used to draft the rubric in line with the learning or assessment goals; to transcribe the IO; to draft feedback for the assessor to review and edit; and to generate a score based on the rubric.

Rather than AI automating instruction or replacing teachers, GAI can be used to scale authentic practice, making it possible to assess personalised learning at scale. This is not mass automated testing but rather an example of using AI to enable a more personalised and authentic approach to assessment that is also scalable, clearly tied to employability and that uses future/transversal skills. Similarly, GAI can be used as a dynamic assessor during a live assessment, where the AI poses the questions, based on the instructors prompts, and student speaks directly to the AI. Again, this is not replacing the instructor but rather enabling the scaling of good assessment practice by using the social affordances of conversational AI.

6.7 Learning as Process

Assessments that measure student learning that can now be completed successfully by AI are no longer fit for purpose, as they cannot reliably demonstrate proof of student learning. Superficial redesign will not be adequate for the challenge ahead because the issue is not whether a generative AI tool can write an essay (for example)—it is whether students can critically conduct and assess research, work through drafts and synthetise information, and apply the lessons they learn from the exercise in another context. That is what is meaningful about the essay assignment and that *process* is where we should focus our efforts. This means that we need to shift our focus from assessing learning as *output* to assessing learning as a *process*. Assessment is part of the learning process (Dann, 2014), it does not exist in isolation from it, so rather than asking students to create or produce an asset or item, it makes more sense to break the project or assignment into its part and assess those parts instead. This means looking at how learning is scaffolded over time and using those steps to design activity-based assessments. For example, the assignment of writing an essay can easily be broken into the various steps, from brainstorming to researching to annotating sources to preparing a draft. There is no reason why instructors cannot assess these steps, just as they teach them in the classroom. The only difference is that rather than focusing on that final piece of output as the means of assessment, we focus on the learning process that leads to creating that output instead.

For instructors who want to ensure an AI-free learning process, the only realistic solution is to flip the classroom and conduct those activities in the presence of the instructor. However, for a truly authentic assessment, it makes more sense to assume that students are using GAI and to incorporate the technology into each of these steps. This could involve any of the steps, from brainstorming topics with AI, to writing and revising a thesis statement with AI, to drafting an outline with AI and editing it, to generating an essay and critiquing its output. At every stage, it is possible to use GAI both as a copilot or assistant but also as a means for critical analysis and learning. Looking beyond the short-term to a time when educators are comfortable integrating GAI into their discipline, it makes more sense to design assessment that builds on the problem-based, inquiry-based, project-based learning approaches we have seen in previous chapters. Those practices, which put learners into the driver's seat and help them to become self-directed learners, can be extended into our assessment practices by using GAI. These active, constructivist approaches offer students the opportunity to demonstrate their learning through more creative and varied means. By using best practices in digital education, such as including grading rubrics for each assignment, instructors can use GAI as collaborator and make the grading of assessments more efficient. Using GAI to draft rubrics, to help grade and to draft feedback can allow educators to use more creative approaches to designing assessments that reflect the active, generative, constructivist and collaborative learning approaches they can design with GAI.

6.7.1 Alternative Assessment

Elkhoury's ten principles of alternative assessment are part of her framework for alternative assessments, which is intended as a starting point for educators looking for ways to move beyond traditional practices and to move peripheral assessment practices into the centre. Alternative assessment, according to their work, should be authentic, equitable, flexible, renewable, interdisciplinary, co-created, continuous, culturally responsive, engaging, and available in alternative forms (Elkhoury, 2023). Her work began with discussions that took place during the Covid-19 pandemic, when many educators were prompted to explore alternative approaches to assessment. "On the surface, educators saw concerns about assessment proctoring and academic integrity. On a deeper level, educators noticed changes related to flexibility, timing and equity. Those conversations paved the way for deeper changes or a paradigm shift. Questions arose: What would higher education look like without exams? What could educators do better, or how could we do it?" (Elkhoury, 2023). The emergency of the pandemic has passed but the education sector has experienced GAI as another crisis to which it is unsure how to respond. But there were valuable lessons learned from the difficult experience of the pandemic, not least the fact that more flexibility is possible, and that digital pedagogies might well be the way forward because they allow us to design sustainable models for this century.

6.8 Human + AI Assessment

The evidence is growing that the division between human versus AI competencies will become less and less useful as GAI capabilities grow, so rather than dividing our list of treasures into AI and human categories, it is more productive to think of AI as *augmenting* our human capabilities. Mollick has written about co-intelligence (Mollick, 2024) and the idea that, when we learn to leverage AI, it will "give us superpowers." Educators should focus on what GAI can do, perhaps better than we can, and how to design learning in collaboration with GAI to capitalise on the strengths on both sides. That is what supercharging our powers means. This is similar to the concept of "intelligence augmentation" or IA, described by Dede et al. in the context of developing judgment skills, as "when AI and humans engage in a complementary partnership in which a human-and-AI team's overall performance is greater than their individual capacity" (Dede et al., 2021). This augmentation of individual intelligence is what we aspire to do when we design learning and assessment with GAI. "One way to achieve IA is through co-creation by humans and AI, where better performance is achieved than when humans work on their own" (Fui-Hoon Nah et al., 2023).

Generativism is grounded in this idea that collaboration with GAI enables us to augment our intelligence by creating learning that is *both* human-centred and AI-powered.

6.8.1 Assessing Content Intelligence: PISA

In July 2023, the OECD published a report on the findings comparing the capabilities of ChatGPT to 15-year-old children across a variety of subject areas (OECD, 2023) which aimed understand the relationship between AI capabilities and human skills in order to suggest policy changes. It tracked how well AI did on the PISA (Programme for International Students) and compared it to students in the core domains of reading, mathematics and science. The report noted that "AI performance is advancing rapidly on tasks that we say require critical and creative thinking when people do them." We can see that the separation into AI versus human skills is gradually disappearing and will not be useful for long. The result is, as described in previous chapters, the new hybrid of humans and AI working in collaboration. Clearly, in the first instance the focus of education needs to shift towards "teaching students how to understand and work with AI systems that outperform them in core areas" (OECD, 2023) because, as we have seen, AI has the power to augment our human competencies. "This does not mean that today's competences will be irrelevant, but it may transform our understanding of which aspects of those competences are most important to emphasise." What does this mean for teaching core competencies? "Specifically, it may require teaching today's competences alongside new competences, emphasising skills like systems-thinking, evaluating and assessing competing claims, commanding and overseeing AI systems, and verifying their outputs." The changes that AI is ushering in will change the competencies we currently teach, "requiring a transformation in our approaches to teaching, pedagogy and assessment." (OECD, 2023).

PISA plans to introduce AI into its performance from 2025. "The assessments would ask students to solve a particular problem in an area where they did not have the requisite foundational knowledge. The students would use AI to help gain the content knowledge." (Klein, 2024) This is the shift from content knowledge to content *intelligence*, from TPACK to TPAIK, described in detail in Chap. 4. "Students would use an AI-powered chatbot to complete their work. They could ask it basic questions about a topic, so that the test could focus on their thinking capability, not whether they possess background knowledge of a particular subject." Students will not need to memorise information because that knowledge is readily available via AI. Instead, students must focus on future skills of problem-solving and critical thinking. This is generativism in action: By using content intelligence, students can jump from memorising information to solving problems. It is also an example of ABC + GAI learning activity Investigation, reframed here as an assessment.

PISA is also experimenting with AI grading in an attempt to discover more about how humans learn. They plans to use AI to score the tests, an idea based on an example from Beijing Normal University, where music students were given half a song and asked to compose the remaining half, and the results were scored by trained musicians and AI. In that case, the AI scores began to match those of the music professionals because the AI learns over time from human experts. Here again we can see AI stepping again into the domain of creativity—though in the guise of a marker—and doing a task that was formerly restricted to humans because of that creative knowledge required. PISA is conducting this experiment on *how* students learn and applying that to the case of performance assessments. Research in neuroscience shows that the human brain can create new synapses for the thoughts that guide our actions. The results could be very important for educators keen to innovate in their assessment types and to learn what AI tells us about the process of learning.

6.8.2 Generative Assessment

The original ABC LD framework provides suggestions for converting analogue activities into digital format. As the PISA experiment shows, such activities can be rethought and converted into generative assessment using GAI as a tool or a presence.

Activity	Analogue	Digital	Generative
Acquisition	Reading books and articles, listening to lectures, watching demonstrations	Using the web, reading digital documents, listening to podcasts, watching videos and animations	GAI feedback and interaction with documents, videos, podcasts
Investigation	Text-based study guides; analysing the ideas and info in a range of resources; using conventional methods to collect and analyse data; comparing texts; searching for and evaluating info and ideas	Using online advice and guidance; analysing the ideas and info in a range of digital resources; comparing digital texts; using digital tools for searching and evaluating information	Generative search and research; GAI-powered analysis and evaluation of texts/resources; GAI for research workflow

(continued)

(continued)

Activity	Analogue	Digital	Generative
Collaboration	Small group projects, discussing peers' outputs, building joint output	Small group project using online fora, wikis, chat rooms; discussing peers' outputs, building a joint digital output	Conversational agents as peers and collaborators; GAI feedback and analysis
Discussion	Tutorials, seminars, discussion groups, class discussions	Online tutorials, seminars, email discussion, online discussion fora, synchronous and asynchronous group web conferencing	Discussion/debate with GAI agents; Socratic dialogue; feedback and skills development
Practice	Practising exercises; doing practice-based projects; labs; field trips; face-to-face role play activities	Using models; simulations; microworlds; virtual labs and field trips; online role play and activities	AI tools for disciplinary practice; generative scenarios; live simulations and role play
Production	Statements; essays; reports; accounts; designs; performances; artefacts; animations; models; videos	Producing and storing digital documents; representations of designs; performances and artefacts; animations; models; resources; slideshows; photos; videos; blogs; eportfolios	Synthetic media co-creation and co-production, co-writing, co-editing, co-creating

6.9 The Agentic Future

Beyond the gates of academe, AI researchers and industries are forging ahead at a whiplash-inducing pace. Partnerships between big tech and the large consulting groups (i.e. Accenture and Anthropic) are a clear sign of the future to come, as companies are equipping the workers of the future to use AI in the workplace. In doing so, industry is actively preparing its workers for the job shifts that are coming. In March 2024, Cognition's autonomous AI coding agent Devin was the first to be able to complete tasks that a junior staff member would normally do. Similar efficiencies across other industries means that junior professionals could well find themselves competing with AIs for work experience. As AI automates a growing number of lower-skilled white-collar jobs that were until recently considered safely under the control of highly educated workers, we must ask: What sorts of assessments do we design for this future? What are the skills and competencies to measure in a human + AI world of work?

We have seen from the misadventures in AI detection that a strategy of exploiting AI's weakness to stay ahead of change is a limited-time offer that is both ineffective and damaging to the relationships at the heart of education. It also misses the point of assessment, which should be about testing competencies and ensuring that students have the skills they need to thrive in this uncertain future. Superficial assessment redesign and short-term stop-gap measures will not be sustainable or adequate for the challenge ahead. Instead of band-aid solutions to conserve existing practices, we need to completely reimagine how we assess learning, starting by revising the outcomes that inform the design of those assessments. Knowledge, skills and competencies—the basic learning outcomes in every course and programme—must be revised for the AI age. The only sustainable option is the new hybrid model of humans working in collaboration with AI.

References

Ardito, C. G. (2023, December 8). Contra generative AI detection in higher education assessments. https://arxiv.org/abs/2312.05241v2. https://doi.org/10.48550/arXiv.2312.05241

Breen, B. (2023, November 14). How to use generative AI for historical research. Res Obscura. Substack blog. https://resobscura.substack.com/p/generative-ai-for-historical-research

Conde, J., Reviriego, P., Salvachúa, A., Martínez, G., Hernández, J. A., & Lombardi, F. (2024, January). Understanding the impact of artificial intelligence in academic writing: metadata to the rescue. *Computer, 57,* 105–109. https://doi.org/10.1109/MC.2023.3327330

Dann, R. (2014). Assessment *as* learning: Blurring the boundaries of assessment and learning for theory, policy and practice. *Assessment in Education: Principles, Policy & Practice, 21*(2), 149–166. https://doi.org/10.1080/0969594X.2014.898128

DCU TEU. Interactive oral assessment. Teaching Enhancement Unit. DCU. https://www.dcu.ie/teu/interactive-oral-assessment

Dede, C., Etemadi, A., & Forshaw, T. (2021). *Intelligence augmentation: Upskilling humans to complement AI.* The Next Level Lab at the Harvard Graduate School of Education. President and Fellows of Harvard College.

Elkhoury, E. (2020). A guide to alternative assessments. York University Teaching Commons. November 2020, updated July 2020. https://www.yorku.ca/teachingcommons/wp-content/uploads/sites/38/2021/07/Guide_alternative_assessments-UPDATED-July-2021.pdf

Elkhoury, E. (2023). Ten principles of alternative assessment. In T. Jaffer, S. Govender, & L. Czerniewicz (Eds.), *Learning design voices.* EdTech Books. https://doi.org/10.59668/279

European Commission. (2023). European digital hub. *AI Squad Briefing Reports 1–4.*

Eaton, S. E. (2023a). Postplagiarism: Transdisciplinary ethics and integrity in the age of artificial intelligence and neurotechnology. *International Journal for Educational Integrity, 19,* 23. https://doi.org/10.1007/s40979-023-00144-1

Eaton, S. E. (2023b, February 23). 6 tenets of postplagiarism: Writing in the age of artificial intelligence. https://drsaraheaton.files.wordpress.com/2023/02/postplagiarism.jpg

Edwards, B. (2023, July 14). Why AI detectors think the US Constitution was written by AI. *Ars Technica.* https://arstechnica.com/information-technology/2023/07/why-ai-detectors-think-the-us-constitution-was-written-by-ai/

Fui-Hoon Nah, F., Zheng, R., Cai, J., Siau, K., & Chen, L. (2023). Generative AI and ChatGPT: Applications, challenges, and AI-human collaboration. *Journal of Information Technology Case and Application Research, 25*(3), 277–304. https://doi.org/10.1080/15228053.2023.2233814

References

Gentile, M., Città, G., Perna, S., & Allegra, M. (2023). Do we still need teachers? Navigating the paradigm shift of the teacher's role in the AI era. *Frontiers in Education, 8*, 1161777. https://doi.org/10.3389/feduc.2023.1161777

Gilbert, D. (2024, February 22). Google's 'Woke' image generator shows the limitations of AI. *Wired*. https://www.wired.com/story/google-gemini-woke-ai-image-generation/

Gray, A. (2024). ChatGPT "contamination": estimating the prevalence of LLMs in the scholarly literature. https://doi.org/10.48550/arXiv.2403.16887. https://arxiv.org/abs/2403.16887v1

Justus, Z., & Janos, N. (2024, March 28). Assessment of student learning is broken. *Inside Higher Ed*. https://www.insidehighered.com/opinion/views/2024/03/28/assessment-student-learning-broken-opinion

Khaleel, K., Harte, P., & Borthwick Saddler, S. (2024, March 1). The financial impact of AI on institutions through breaches of academic integrity. HEPI blog. https://www.hepi.ac.uk/2024/03/01/the-financial-impact-of-ai-on-institutions-through-breaches-of-academic-integrity/

Klein, A. (2024, March 25). AI may be coming for standardized testing. *Education Week*. https://www.edweek.org/teaching-learning/ai-may-be-coming-for-standardized-testing/2024/03

Lee, S. (2023). *AI literacy competency framework for educators*. Paradox Learning. https://paradoxlearning.com/wp-content/uploads/2024/01/AI-Literacy-Competency-Framework-for-Educator_new-1.pdf. https://paradoxlearning.com/resources/

Liang, W., Zhang, Y., Wu, Z., Lepp, H., Ji, W., Zhao, X., Cao, H., Liu, S., He, S., Huang, Z., Yang, D., Potts, C., Manning, C. D., & Zou, J. Y. (2024, April 1). Mapping the increasing use of LLMs in scientific papers. https://doi.org/10.48550/arXiv.2404.01268. https://arxiv.org/abs/2404.01268

Logan, D., & Sotiriadou, P. (n.d.). Interactive oral assessments: A viable model for COVID-19 and beyond. *Griffith University Enlighten*. https://enlighten.griffith.edu.au/interactive-oral-assessments-a-viable-model-for-covid-19-and-beyond/

Mishra, P., Warr, M., & Islam, R. (2023). TPACK in the age of ChatGPT and generative AI. *Journal of Digital Learning in Teacher Education, 39*(4), 235–251. https://doi.org/10.1080/21532974.2023.2247480

Mollick, E. (2022, July 15). How to use AI to do stuff: An opinionated guide. One Useful Thing. Substack blog. https://www.oneusefulthing.org/p/how-to-use-ai-to-do-stuff-an-opinionated

Mollick, E. (2024). *Co-intelligence: Living and working with AI*. Penguin.

OECD. (2023). Putting AI to the test: How does the performance of GPT and 15-year-old students in PISA compare? OECD Education Spotlights. Directorate for Education and Skills.

Perkins, M., Furze, L., Roe, J., & McVaughan, J. (2023, 2024). The artificial intelligence assessment scale (AIAS): A framework for ethical integration of generative AI in educational assessment. *Journal of University Teaching and Learning Practice, 21*(06). https://doi.org/10.53761/q3azde36

Pigg, S. (2024). Research writing with ChatGPT: A descriptive embodied practice framework. *Computers and Composition, 71*, 102830, ISSN 8755-4615. https://doi.org/10.1016/j.compcom.2024.102830

Scott, K., & Bonar, M. (2024, February 28). Glasgow University students' anger over reintroduction of in-person exams. *BBC*. https://www.bbc.co.uk/news/uk-scotland-glasgow-west-68380264

Skilton, M., & Hovsepian, F. (2018). *The 4th industrial revolution: Responding to the impact of artificial intelligence on business*. Palgrave Macmillan. https://doi.org/10.1007/978-3-319-62479-2

Soffel, J. (2016, March 10). Ten 21st-century skills every student needs. *World Economic Forum*. https://www.weforum.org/agenda/2016/03/21st-century-skills-future-jobs-students/

Susnjak, T. (2022, December 19). ChatGPT: The end of online exam integrity? https://doi.org/10.48550/arXiv.2212.09292. https://arxiv.org/abs/2212.09292v1

Weber, T. (2024, March 19). Inside the AI competition that decoded an ancient Herculaneum Scroll. *Scientific American.* https://www.scientificamerican.com/article/inside-the-ai-competition-that-decoded-an-ancient-scroll-and-changed/

Young, J. R. (2024, April 4). What happened after this college student's paper was falsely flagged for AI use after using Grammarly. *Fast Company.* https://www.fastcompany.com/91074029/can-using-grammarly-set-off-ai-detection-software

Chapter 7
Embedding AI

Abstract This chapter discusses the integration of generative AI into institutional planning and design, and considers the implications in terms of changes to processes, modes and ways of working by looking at the spatial, cultural, and structural implications of such a shift. It closes with a short list of actions for educators and administrators to begin.

Keywords Embedding AI · AI ethics · Institutional planning · Digital transformation · Digital infrastructure · Digital equity and accessibility · Human-centred AI · Learning agility · Communities of practice

7.1 Introduction

Innovation gurus in the early 2000s used to talk about the "VUCA" (volatile, unstable, uncertain, complex) world, using it as a catch-all phrase for "it's crazy out there!" (Bennett & Lemoine, 2014) to call on leaders to cultivate resilience in infrastructure, people and systems and enable them to withstand the effects of disruption. Throughout 2022, education technology experts warned about the disruption that AI would bring (Sharples, 2022, 2022a, 2022b; Sharples & Perez, 2022) but those warnings fell on deaf ears and when the tsunami arrived, education as a sector was unprepared. A year later, after several letters and warnings about the potential existential risk posed by prominent voices in AI, including Geoff Hinton and the Future of Life Institute, two important events took place: First, the firing (and rehiring) of Sam Altman as CEO of OpenAI, which brought the discussion about the risks posed by the pace of development of GAI into mainstream media; and second, the EU, USA, UK and G7 countries acted in quick succession to meet and issue principles and to discuss legislation to control that pace and the direction of development. Governments have since worked to regulate the development of GAI to ensure it does not pose a danger to human wellbeing. The EU passed the EU AI Act, ensuring that the use of AI technologies including facial recognition and emotion detection were forbidden, while all use of AI in education was classified as high-risk. Far from a passing fad, GAI has become the most important agenda item for government leaders.

GAI has also gone mainstream in industry (Scriven, 2023) and the impact on the workplace is clear. A 2023 Microsoft study on workers using its Copilot productivity tools showed they completed tasks 26 to 73% faster than without them (Cambon et al., 2023) and a Harvard study the same year showed consultants with access to GPT-4 worked 25% faster and experienced a 40% quality improvement (Dell'Acqua et al., 2023). Meanwhile, GAI has continued to improve in terms of capabilities. Stanford's Institute for Human-Centred Artificial Intelligence (HAI) *2024 AI Index* indicated that AI could match or exceed human capabilities in tasks including reading comprehension, image classification and competition-level mathematics (Stanford, 2024), painting a picture of artificial intelligence that is certain to have an increasing impact on our knowledge economy and knowledge workers.

Education, slow at first to react, also kicked into gear. But while guidelines have been issued reiterating the high-level principles about safety and responsibility to which educators and student should adhere, there has been little forthcoming in terms of how educators can actually use GAI in their teaching or—importantly - what the implications are of this sea change for the model of education. Academic staff alone cannot drive these changes—the systemic challenges posed by GAI require a systemic response. Integrating GAI requires support from the top. Leaders need to guide the process of integrating generative AI into their institution. Educators need access to frontier models, training to use them, and time redesign their courses. Leaders must initiate and support the development of AI literacy for students and provide guidance on the use of AI tools in their work, so that they are equipped to both critically evaluate and use AI responsibly, as well as prepared to take up roles in an AI-powered workplace. They must provide a path for the educational development of academic and professional staff, as well as students. They need to take a proactive and sustainable approach, informed by the values and mission of education.

7.2 AI Ethics

There are clear ethical issues to be confronted when discussing the integration of GAI into educational institutions, not least the training data, the biases in the system, the corporate backing, and the energy required to power it. Clear limitations must guide and restrict the use of GAI in education. These limits have raised by national and international bodies, passed into law by the European Union and outlined in detail by UNESCO. These actions and recommendations are a direct response to the loud and persistent warnings from vocal opponents of the current approach to GAI development, including Gary Marcus and Geoff Hinton. They must be heeded. There are many reasons to be skeptical, not least some of the more ominous motivations that have driven AI research and development (Popenici, 2023). We are living in a period of vast inequality, of upheaval and increased violence, of xenophobia and racism. GAI as it currently exists is deeply flawed, demonstrably biased and not representative of the diversity of populations or multitude of voices in our world. The energy use required to train AI models and generate output is out of all proportion to what we can afford given our current resource challenges and the climate crisis that has gripped our planet. These are the clear and present dangers of GAI.

But AI is also everywhere and to ignore it would be negligent. Geoff Hinton said in an interview with *Times Higher Education*, that AI without the humanities leads to events like the genocide of the Uighurs because creates a technocratic society that lacks fundamental human values (Baker, 2021). This is not the future we want. AI offers great promise for research and discovery, to provide scientific breakthroughs, to make learning more accessible, to unlock creativity, to ease our burdens, to change our world for the better. But for technology to serve us humans, we must learn about how it works from the inside and understand its output, so that we can be informed users, commentators and critics. This is the critical AI literacy that staff and students alike need, to help steer the future direction of development. It is only by engaging directly with GAI, by using the inquiry-based approaches suggested in this book, that they can learn those skills.

Like all technology, AI is a double-edged sword and we must approach it as such. Dron argues that the use of GAI can and will change us as a species (Dron, 2023). For that change to be a positive one, in the direction of intelligence *augmentation* rather than automation, we need to engage constructively with GAI, to engage in critical thinking, to augment rather than stifle creativity, to refine our collaboration skills, to increase our understanding of the world. It is precisely GAI's flawed nature that provides educators with such clear opportunities to meaningfully engage, to help students think critically, to dig deeply and to construct meaning—to make sense, in the way that generative learning is designed to do. Those skills, developed through the active, generative, constructivist, social, collaborative approaches described in throughout this book, are the key to unlocking the human skills that students need to successfully navigate this world. Educators can design learning with GAI that serves this mission but to do so they need to understand it, so that they can use it constructively, and so that ultimately they and their students can use is as a force for good (Czerniewicz & Cronin, 2023; Pechenkina, 2023).

7.3 Institutional Context

Technology alone will not change anything. Indeed, "expecting technology to transform education is to give technological tools far more agency than they actually have" (Mishra et al., 2023). This is the narrative that we have seen from industry, the mistaken idea that AI will magically transform a broken system. Those actually working in education know this is not the case. Indeed, the industry narrative "ignores the fact that these tools operate within, and gain their meaning from, broader social structures and systems of education, which have not changed." Education is a vast and slow-moving system, bound by deep layers of bureaucratic red tape. It is the exact opposite of industry, which is why the stand-off between industry and academia is so unproductive. "Not only are these structures inherently UN-agile, they are also conservative by nature. This is particularly important in the context of new technologies, such as GenAI, which has significant potential to disrupt exsisting systems and practice" (Mishra et al., 2023). The bottom line for education is that it is the institutional context that determines the pace, nature and scale of change. And so, it is at the institutional level that real change must happen.

The ongoing and uneven process of digital transformation that has been underway in education for many years but the degree of progress varies widely. While most industries *have* digitally transformed—we see this all around us in the apps and tools we use to shop, eat, travel—education is the exception. Indeed, many educational institutions have yet to begin the journey of coming to grips with Web 2.0 digital technologies, so adding Web 4.0 and AI to the to-do list is very daunting. We can see the scale of the challenge clearly on many campuses, where the digital and technological infrastructure fall far behind the physical spaces where people work and learn. In effect, this means that the ability to offer blended delivery, flexible spaces for teaching or collaborative spaces for learning—not to mention the technologies those spaces require—is very limited.

In short, education lags far behind industry standards in all aspects of digital transformation, including both the technological and digital infrastructure needed to support it—so while Web 4.0 technology exists beyond the classroom, the physical and digital infrastructure to support Education 4.0 are often not in place. This means that traditional education needs to now perform a leap-frog manoeuvre, transitioning from a mostly analogue model with a bit of digital on the side to an AI-enabled model of education. But it is unreasonable and unrealistic to expect educators to update their teaching practices for the world of AI when the institution in which they teach is still working towards an analogue model. Institutional leaders ugently need to address this technological and digital infrastructure gap if they are to offer a sustainable model of education that meets the needs of our emerging AI-driven economy.

Educators as a group can also be very conservative when it comes to the adoption of new technologies (Bates et al., 2020; Bećirović, 2023) and the initial response to the launch of ChatGPT-3.5 illustrated this dramatically. Meanwhile, leaders tend to be high-level administrators with institutional management skills but often little direct knowledge of learning technologies or design. A combination of an overabundance of caution, combined with the the academic tendency to wait for proof of positive outcomes before experimenting, meant that education fell further behind at precisely the time when movement was needed. But the early debate about whether or not to adopt GAI is over. It is in our enterprise systems, devices and the software we use every day, and there is no doubt about its critical importance to the future of work.

The narrative in education around GAI sometimes confuses this technology with previous examples of digital tools and the platformisation of education in particular. The antipathy towards all things "edtech" caused many to initially write GAI off as a fad or trend that would quickly die down. The conversation around GAI—and particularly ChatGPT, which tends to be used a synonyn for GAI—has therefore confused GAI with the digital tools of the Web 2.0 era. The spectre of the increasing platformisation of education in particular is a topic that crops up regularly. Many academics have had a bad experience with edtech integration and they are wary of more of the same happening with AI. The framing of GAI as a calculator—or "just another tool" to add to the teaching kit—has not helped create a good understanding of the significance of GAI for education.

But to be clear: GAI is no more an edtech tool than the internet is. It is an all-purpose technology that can be used in a multitude of ways. And looking beyond the classroom, the significance of GAI is clearly much greater. Put simply, the world is changing rapidly and we need to change with it in order to serve our students. That is, after all, the mission of education. "We must continually ask ourselves what is truly important for our students to know so that they are prepared for an unpredictable and emerging future, in which AI technologies will lead to job transformation and economic change" (Mishra et al., 2023). In the age of human–computer integration, our students need the digital/AI skills to thrive in this labour market and the content intelligence to work directly with AI in their chosen field. But for this to happen, educators need pedagogical intelligence, which means the design skills and the digital and AI competence to work directly with GAI to create educational experiences. The best way to inculcate those skills is to design learning activities in collaboration with GAI. Indeed, the real difference between GAI and the platform model of edtech is that engaging with GAI—using the new hybrid model—puts the power to create directly into the hands of educators.

7.4 Institutional Priorities

Most, if not all, highly ranked institutions are structured to foster and promote research, and university ratings are largely determined by that research output. Lecturers are hired from Ph.D. programmes or postdocs for their disciplinary expertise and research skills, though there are, of course, other non-traditional paths to academia, such as from the professions, but these are not the norm. Once inside the academy, lecturers are there primarily to conduct research and to teach. The ratios of research to teaching differs depending on the role and the institution but in most cases, those hired in research positions focus on the research quality, quantity and impact, while those hired in teaching positions focus on classroom delivery. Some in the latter category produce scholarship, often directly related to their teaching activities, but the expectations of the institution on them is not the same.

While a growing number of institutions encourage excellence in teaching and learning, this is still generally viewed as a secondary activity, and innovation in teaching is not rewarded in the same way as research. There is therefore a disconnect at present in terms of what the tertiary-level educator is hired to do and what they are trained to do. But pedagogical innovation is now a critical imperative for all institutions, so educators must have time to invest in experimentation, testing and sharing. GAI can assist by reducing the time spent on some aspects of a typical academic's workload and freeing up time for more potentially productive pursuits but ultimately this is a structural issue that must be addressed at the highest level. Roles will change with GAI integration and some tasks will become much less time intensive than they have been historically. These efficiency gains must be fed back into the system to support redesign and make educational offerings more sustainable.

7.5 Teaching Spaces

Historically, when thinking about educational delivery, we have had two options—face-to-face or online, plus a more recently a third, a blend of the two. Now, learning can happen anywhere the AI ecosystem exists, which means the classroom is everywhere. This is a significant shift for education. For traditional education, university has been a physical place where students go, not just to attend class, but to live and make friends and grow as a person over a period of years. But times have changed. The cost of education, the cost of living, the need to upskill and reskill, the need for more accessible and affordable education, have meant that online learning has expanded globally and on campuses, blended delivery is rapidly becoming the most popular modality. Walk around any campus today and it is clear that students, while technically and physically on campus, are simultaneously occupying virtual worlds. Connected classrooms can be used to "foster inter-group collaboration and resource sharing, overcoming the boundaries and limitations of the traditional classroom through the Internet and the cloud" (Gentile et al., 2023). GAI enables educational delivery to become much more flexible, to take place in virtual spaces and on devices using GAI tools. The Metaverse Film School is a virtual space where students can learn skills in Virtual Reality (VR). As VR becomes generative, the potential for learning skills in the Metaverse will increase, enabling learning using real-time generative simulations. Similarly, the integration of GAI into robotics will bring these capabilities to embodied AI. Web 4.0 tools and the Internet of Things will enable us to extend the classroom far beyond the physical confines of campus and create new spaces for learning with AI experts of all shapes and forms.

7.6 Covid Lessons

Over the last two decades, online learning sector has led the charge in terms of digital innovation. From MOOCs to micro credentials, online education for non-traditional students paved the way for mainstream education. Meanwhile, most large universities continued to focus on campus-based instruction. Digital learning has been seen as something separate from the norm, left to campus elearning teams to develop rather than for educators to design, while lecturers focus on the 'real' (i.e., physical) classroom. University-based elearning teams have also tended historically to employ learning technologists, who advise on the implementation of a tool, rather than learning designers, who advise on the pedagogical approach throughout the full course design cycle. During the Covid-19 pandemic, the cost of this omission in professional development for academic staff became clear, as we witnessed what can happen when technology is implemented hurriedly and without design. There was a massive increase in demand for instructional designers, as universities grappled with the challenges of switching to online provision with little to no in-house expertise, and many educators and their students learned the hard way that simply moving in-person teaching online does not work. This was, in part, what made the Covid pandemic such a stressful event for academic staff: They were never trained for teach online and their courses were never designed for online delivery. It would be short-sighted to ignore the lesson from the Covid crisis, as it has a direct bearing on what institutions are now grappling with as they struggle to deal with GAI. Despite two decades of efforts, recent research shows that the vast majority of educators are still not digitally competent (Bećirović, 2023). They do not receive the necessary training to leverage digital tools, nor are they skilled in digital learning design. They are therefore ill-equipped to deal with a new and disruptive technology in their classrooms. Critically, they have not be trained in instructional design for digital environments. But all education is now digital—indeed, soon to be AI—so it is urgent that educators become compenent in these areas.

7.7 Experimentation

Designing digitally enabled courses requires a robust cycle of piloting, testing and evaluation, and pilots of GAI tools require safety and risk assessment, ethical clearance, and user consent, unless the institution is using a closed system. Educational institutions are notoriously slow when it comes to procuring new technologies, so agile processes are also needed to access technology and create pilots that support experimentation, so that staff and students can experiment safely with tools. Ideally, institutions should also build their own tools on private LLMs. Open-source models and tools are just as good as the proprietary frontier models, so where the human resources exist to do so it makes sense to explore this option. Where that is not an option, small project teams should be allocated budgets and given the power to make decisions for themselves, so they can test, iterate, and share their results with others. To do this, institutions need to plan for more flexible team structures, where staff collaborate on a project and then move to another. Not only is this a positive move for fostering collegiality, it also enourages staff to foster connections outside of one's disciplinary area with staff working in other fields. It raises the profile of professional staff teaching and learning staff, and elearning teams, as they work alongside academics in the creation of courses, sharing expertise as equals. In an example of team-based design (Vaughan & Garrison, 2006), academic staff in different areas formed a Community of Inquiry to create courses for blended delivery. Sharing their progress, testing and iterating as they went, this exemplifies the collaborative, team-based approach to blended learning design. These are the sorts of agile, collaborative approaches to design that GAI requires.

7.8 Transformation

Embedding GAI will transform not just teaching, learning, research and assessment, but also all of the administrative functions that support an educational institution, so institutions need to plan for change and continued disruption. Unlike the Covid-19 pandemic, this disruption is not a short-term event. Instead, this is the beginning of a larger and more extended disruption that will expand and grow over the next decade. From recruitment to enrolment to retention, at every stage and in every administrative process, GAI will change how we work. Collaborative learning design implies a shift to a team-based approach; delivery of the new hybrid model requires robust digital and IT infrastructure; assessment as learning requires updating ingrained administrative processes. The systemic challenges posed by AI require a systemic response and integrating GAI requires support from the top. Academics alone cannot use GAI without institutional support in the form of funding for technology, support for training, and support for the large-scale and ongoing shifts that need to happen.

The model of education must change to support an AI-enabled, agile, flexible, and competency-focused approach to education that will be sustainable in the AI world. We need to shift to new model that incorporates the new hybrid of human + AI, where class activities are active, generative, social, constructivist learning, and dynamic, authentic and generative assessments are distributed over the term. Integrating GAI will take significant investment in upskilling of academic staff, which requires support from the top, in the form of institutional planning and investment; in changes to administrative processes and ways of working; and in support for new digital and physical infrastructure. "Integrating technologies into education is a joint rather than an individual endeavour… [that] involves policymakers, educational management, teachers, parents and students." (Bećirović, 2023). Some of the key strategies for the implementation of digital technologies are already underway at many institutions, including issuing guidance for use. What remains to be created are the policies and guidance to actually *integrate* this technology into the teaching and learning process; financial support for these activities; access to hardware and software, specifically subscriptions to frontier models and other tools; training on the ethical use of GAI and AI literacy.

But at the highest level, GAI integration requires an institutional vision for change, a culture that embraces experimentation, and the support to bring it to life. Changing the culture and giving people the time and support they need to design and create is critical. Without that vision, culture change and support, nothing will change. All of the physical and infrastructure in the world will not help if educators do not have the time and space to innovate, test, share and co-create. Institutional leaders must support their educators in this journey.

7.9 Embedding AI

Embedding AI requires action on several fronts but the key actions and mindsets need to begin are:

1. Embrace learning agility: Agility is the most important competency for educators, as they grapple with GAI. A minimum of 10 hours of experimentation is the average before users begin to appreciate the ways that working with GAI can transform practice.
2. Provide access: Access to frontier AI models for all should be a priority for every institution. Subscriptions are expensive so working with other institutions is advised. Building in-house systems is another option for institutions with the funds to support it.
3. Create an AI network: Every department needs an AI lead, to liaise with senior leadership, connect them to activities on the ground, and be the source of information for colleagues.
4. Form a community of practice of innovators, testers and mentors: Educators can learn from each other's experiments, successes and failures. Set up a digital space to share those experiments, so that others can follow that lead. Curation is more efficient than creation.
5. Embed digital pedagogies built on evidence-based practice: Integration of GAI into teaching and learning must be pedagogy-first. Brush up on learning theory and digital pedagogy, take an online course in digital learning design with/for AI.
6. Share best practices in AI-informed learning design to upskill staff: Share the best and most useful examples with your network so everyone can benefit. Inspiration will follow!
7. Use the AI ecosystem of tools to rethink and redesign activities: Flip the classroom for any activities that have to be "no AI" and use class time for high-value activities like sense-making with a group.
8. Reframe assessment as learning: Rethink assessment, starting with the learning activities from the ABC + GAI exercises and consider how to use GAI to make those into dynamic assessments.

When it comes to integrating GAI into education, we are only restricted by our imaginations. The aim of this book has been to provide a place to start on that journey of discovery.

References

Baker, S. (2021, September 1). Tech without humanities 'ends in situations like that of Uighers'. *Times Higher Education.* https://www.timeshighereducation.com/news/tech-without-humanities-ends-situations-uighurs

Bates, T., Cobo, C., & Mariño, O., et al. (2020). Can artificial intelligence transform higher education? *International Journal of Educational Technology in Higher Education, 17*, 42. https://doi.org/10.1186/s41239-020-00218-x

Bećirović, S. (2023). *Digital pedagogy: The use of digital technologies in contemporary education.* Springer. https://doi.org/10.1007/978-981-99-0444-0

Bennett, N., & Lemoine, G. J. (2014). What VUCA really means for you. *Harvard Business Review.* https://hbr.org/2014/01/what-vuca-really-means-for-you

Cambon, et al. (2023). *Early LLM-based tools for enterprise information workers likely provide meaningful boosts to productivity.* Microsoft. AI and Productivity. https://www.microsoft.com/en-us/research/uploads/prod/2023/12/AI-and-Productivity-Report-First-Edition.pdf

Czerniewicz, L., & Cronin, C. (Eds.) (2023). *Higher education for good: Teaching and learning futures.* Open Book Publishers. https://doi.org/10.11647/OBP.0363

Dell'Acqua, F., McFowland III, E., Mollick, E., Lifshitz-Assaf, H., Kellogg, K. C., Rajendran, S., Krayer, L., Candelon, F., & Lakhani, K. R. (2023). *Navigating the jagged technological frontier: Field experimental evidence of the effects of AI on knowledge worker productivity and quality.* Harvard Business School Technology & Operations Mgt. Unit Working Paper No. 24-013, Available at SSRN: https://ssrn.com/abstract=4573321 or https://doi.org/10.2139/ssrn.4573321

Dron, J. (2023). The human nature of generative AIs and the technological nature of humanity: Implications for education. *Digital, 3*, 319–335. https://doi.org/10.3390/digital3040020

Gentile, M., Città, G., Perna, S., & Allegra, M. (2023). Do we still need teachers? Navigating the paradigm shift of the teacher's role in the AI era. *Frontiers in Education, 8*, 1161777. https://doi.org/10.3389/feduc.2023.1161777

Lee, S. (2023). *AI literacy competency framework for educators.* Paradox Learning.

Mishra, P., Warr, M., & Islam, R. (2023). TPACK in the age of ChatGPT and generative AI. *Journal of Digital Learning in Teacher Education, 39*(4), 235–251. https://doi.org/10.1080/21532974.2023.2247480

Pechenkina, E. (2023). Artificial intelligence for good? Challenges and possibilities of AI in higher education from a justice perspective. In L. Cerniewicz, & C. Cronin (Eds.), *Higher education for good: Teaching and learning futures.*

Popenici, S. (2023). *Artificial intelligence and learning futures.* Routledge.

Scriven, G. (2023, November 13). AI will go mainstream in 2024. *The Economist.* https://www.economist.com/the-world-ahead/2023/11/13/generative-ai-will-go-mainstream-in-2024

Sharples, M. (2022a, May 17). New AI tools that can write student essays require educators to rethink teaching and assessment [Blog post]. https://blogs.lse.ac.uk/impactofsocialsciences/2022/05/17/new-ai-tools-that-can-write-student-essays-require-educators-to-rethink-teaching-and-assessment/

Sharples, M. (2022b, June 7). AI now writes essays, how might teachers respond? [Blog post]. https://blogs.lse.ac.uk/highereducation/2022/06/09/ai-now-writes-essays-how-might-teachers-respond/

Sharples, M., & Perez, R. G. (2022, September 7). Transform learning with AI [Blog post]. https://blogs.lse.ac.uk/highereducation/2022/09/07/transforming-the-classroom-with-ai/

References

Stanford Institute for Human-Centred Artificial Intelligence. (2024). *Artificial intelligence index.* https://aiindex.stanford.edu/report/

Vaughan, N. D., & Garrison, R. (2006). "How blended learning can support a faculty development community of inquiry." *Online Learning, 10*(4).

SPRINGER NATURE

GPSR Compliance

The European Union's (EU) General Product Safety Regulation (GPSR) is a set of rules that requires consumer products to be safe and our obligations to ensure this.

If you have any concerns about our products, you can contact us on ProductSafety@springernature.com

In case Publisher is established outside the EU, the EU authorized representative is:

Springer Nature Customer Service Center GmbH
Europaplatz 3
69115 Heidelberg, Germany

The manufacturer's authorised representative in the EU is Springer Nature Customer Service Centre GmbH, Europaplatz 3, 69115 Heidelberg, Germany. If you have any concerns regarding our products, please contact ProductSafety@springernature.com

Printed and bound by CPI Group (UK) Ltd, Croydon, CR0 4YY

25/03/2026

02078172-0018